Journey to Nowhere

Journey to Nowhere

One Woman Looks for the Promised Land

EVA FIGES

Granta Books
London

Granta Publications, 12 Addison Avenue, London W11 4QR

First published in Great Britain by Granta Books, 2008

PROLOGUE

I am a grandmother now and, like all grandmothers, I have a head full of stories about the past. But my stories are not like other people's, which makes them more fascinating for my descendants, if not always easy to talk about. All of them are strange, in one way or another, but so were the times.

I was born in Berlin a few months before Hitler came to power, and my family were secular Jews. So, apart from an aunt who followed us to London a few weeks later in the summer of 1939, I would never see any of those faces from my brief Berlin childhood again.

All except one.

Her name was Edith, and I had not thought about her in years, not consciously anyhow, until one afternoon when I was driving down Lisson Grove with my son and his family. He and his wife were on their way to a Chelsea football match at Stamford Bridge, while I was sitting in the back with their twin daughters. They were going to drop us off at the V&A, to see a new exhibition, when I leaned forward. Ahead of us was the Marylebone Road, and a red-brick frontage: the Samaritan Free Hospital for Women and Children. Even the lettering had been removed, since what was left of the building had not been used as a hospital for decades.

Did I ever tell you the story of Edith? I asked, remembering how I had once been to the hospital to visit her. The last time I saw her, and the only time I had ever been in the building. It was the year that the NHS came into being, and I suppose the late Victorian building was already considered obsolete.

No, of course I had not told my family about Edith. After all, she was only a minor character in the history of my family. Our housemaid, back in the Tauenzienstrasse, which we left for the last time on a bleak March morning of 1939. Was she even there when the front door of our apartment clanged shut for the last time? I doubt it. It was a traumatic morning and the whole family were distressed in their different ways. I was on the verge of hysteria at the thought of not seeing my grandparents one last time, and my father seemed anxious to get out of Berlin before someone came to arrest him yet again. There were painful, final goodbyes to be said, not least to the city itself. Who would have spared a thought for the housemaid, even though she had been with us for years?

But the angle of vision changes with time, and at that moment, driving down Lisson Grove half a century later, Edith's story suddenly seemed worth telling. Just because it went against the grain, the in-built prejudices of a lifetime. About Germans, and Germany, for a start, and all the mixed emotions that went with a background like mine.

I doubt whether I gave more than the briefest of outlines before the Victorian façade of the old hospital was left behind. I think there was a short discussion on the quickest route to the V&A, but I knew that I was going to try and tell Edith's story, even though I did not know how it ended. She had simply disappeared, as so many had done before her, leaving no trace.

At the time that I got to know her again, in post-war London, my main concern was to help her find some niche in the world where she could be happy, or at least content. Now that she is beyond all help I owe her a debt I cannot repay, except by dedicating this book to her. Humble Edith, who never asked much of life and got less. Because in the process of researching this book I have had to reassess many things.

Firstly the predicament of the German people, caught up in a reign of terror – this was relatively easy, since even as a schoolgirl I had asked myself (and my father) just what we would have done if we had not been Jewish. My parents were decent human beings but not, I think, heroes. Heroism of a sort was forced upon them.

Secondly, and more importantly, I had to find out about the creation of Israel. Coming from a family of secular Jews, I had been mildly interested, but also bewildered, by the apparent euphoria that greeted the event. Why had Edith chosen to go there, at great risk to herself, when – as a German citizen – she was entitled to massive compensation, only to leave after a brief period of disillusion?

What I discovered during the process of my researches appalled me. I have always thought that the creation of Israel was a catastrophic mistake, perhaps the worst of the twentieth century. I have also, always, had doubts about Israel's right to exist, unless the Jews managed to hold the moral high ground, which they have signally failed to do. However, I did not expect to find out that the creation of Israel was the result, not of global remorse, but of continuing anti-Semitism. The main culprit in this sorry story was of course the United States, with President Truman at the helm.

To Edith, then, I dedicate this story of survival, and the sorrow it so often brings. To Edith and thousands of others, who were betrayed by the victors of a terrible war, and who were expected to fight for a homeland most of them did not even want.

ONE

Those post-war years were a time of new beginnings, when fractured lives had somehow to be patched up. For a family like ours, who had fled Hitler's Germany in the spring of 1939, the challenges were specific: to build a future in a new country and forget the old. There was no going back, and there was nobody to go back to. A few of our relatives were scattered across the world, the rest were dead. There were no graves, no death certificates, but we knew. An unspoken rule in our household was silence: we did not speak about the dead, exactly how and where they had died. Lying awake in the dark, I was free to imagine alternative endings, each one more awful than the last. It was not a good way to cope with loss of this sort. Perhaps there is no good way to deal with it.

Outwardly, by 1947, decisions had been made, new norms established. My father was out of the army and we had, during the famously awful winter of that year, moved out of our rented flat and into a semi-detached house we could call our own. My father was working in the rag trade, my brother was a day boy at Highgate School and I, still at the same grammar school, simply had a longer bus journey

———

to get home. The whole family had been 'naturalized' in the summer of 1946, so we were British now. We were staying. Letters arrived from relatives and friends, survivors of the old world in Berlin. The stamps, from the USA, from Europe, went into my father's collection. At Christmas an aunt of my father's sent grapefruit from Palestine. An 'Aryan' relative by marriage sent *Stollen* to remind us of the old home on Christmas Eve. It was a time of year we would always celebrate in the German fashion, but we were staying. In Hendon, NW11.

Most of the people who wrote or even came to visit us in our new home were people I did not know, had not even heard of in my early childhood, back in pre-war Berlin. The first years of life are narrow and close. But one person from that now unreachable and distant time did unexpectedly get in touch, and her letter to my mother got me very excited. Edith had written to ask for her old job back.

I could scarcely believe it. Edith had been our housemaid in that other world which had been so utterly destroyed. In her own way she had been very important in my young life, as servants so often were in those days. I had a nursemaid then, but I probably spent as much time with Edith as I did with my mother, one way and another. So when my mother told me that Edith had written, and was coming, I did not ask, Edith who? Come to think of it, I never did know her surname, either then or later.

———

―――

Edith was coming. Edith was coming home. She had found us after all these years. Apparently she had gone to Palestine, the new Israel, but was unhappy. Our new home had a small spare bedroom, so she could come. For me, nothing so exciting had happened in a long time, and I still remember my sense of expectancy during the weeks of waiting. I would poke my head round the door of the spare room, facing the street on the first-floor landing, next door to my parents' room, to see how the preparations were going. My first sense of unease began then, when I saw how little was being done.

Edith was a humble person, with low expectations. Brought up in an orphanage, she slept in a dark slip of a room next to our Berlin kitchen. I never saw her in anything but her black and white maid's uniform. No make-up, no jewellery, very few possessions for me to look at when she let me into her room during time off, patiently answering my childish questions.

But now I was no longer that six-year-old innocent, I was an adolescent who had been profoundly changed by the cataclysmic events of the past decade. Then, I was a bewildered child unable to understand why her familiar world was falling apart. Now, I wore an English school uniform and spoke English most of the time, and I knew only too well why we had left Germany in such haste.

I was not the only person who had changed in those

―――

———

years. It is not possible to step twice into the same river, especially a river as dark and deep as the one we had crossed in the last decade. I dreamt of it sometimes, the old world. Always the same dream: the day of departure, a grey March morning, small figures waving from the edge of the airfield as we waited for the plane to take off. After which I woke up, put on my school uniform as usual and got on with being the person I was now, a bright grammar-school girl with an interest in languages, art and literature. Scholarship material, they said.

As a family we did talk about the past: the happy times. Skiing holidays, sailing on the Havel at weekends, idyllic summer days in the weekend house with its garden and the biggest cherry tree in the world. The other stuff was not mentioned. I knew my father had nightmares about his time in Dachau, but nothing would induce him to talk about it. My need to know what had happened to my maternal grandfather and his wife was matched by my mother's need not to know, so she took refuge in silence and, occasionally, improbable lies.

So I think I knew more clearly than either Edith or my mother that we had all changed during the war years. The furniture, much of it brought from Berlin, might look the same, life might seem as though it was getting back to normal, but that was a delusion. I knew from personal experience that my mother was no longer the kind, gentle

———

woman of my early childhood, but a difficult, embittered one. I also knew instinctively that Edith, after everything she had been through, was not just looking for her old job back. Quite alone in the world, she needed to be part of a family now that the nightmare was over, and we were obviously that family. As far as I was concerned Edith was coming home, but the spartan little room made me realize that my mother did not see it that way. She was getting her house-maid back: another welcome sign of returning normality. One of the many problems with my mother was that one could never tell her what she was doing wrong. There would have been a row, I knew. So I kept quiet, but I felt uneasy about the situation.

My most vivid memories of Edith in Berlin concern the period from Kristallnacht in early November 1938 to our departure a few months later, in the following March. It was a time when all the normal household routines were suspended, and I was often left to my own devices, in the rather absent-minded care of our two live-in servants, Edith and my nursemaid, always referred to as Schwester Eva in the formal fashion of the period. It has to be remembered that under the race laws enacted in 1935 Jewish families could only employ Jewish domestics, so Edith and Schwester Eva had their own preoccupations, and a bit of neglect was hardly surprising.

I remember it as a confused, bewildering and tedious time. Since the apartheid system also applied to education, I was not allowed to go to a normal German school, and after 9 November all so-called 'Jewish' schools, many of which had sprung up as a result of the 1935 decrees, closed their doors for safety reasons. My mother did not even attempt to send me to school via the tram that ran along our street, but I have since learnt that the headmistress, with

———

tears in her eyes, instructed all the children who did turn up on the 10th to go home and not return. Many parents had of course telephoned for instructions, and been told not to send their children in.

So there I was, having only embarked on my school career a few months earlier (German children begin school at the age of six, with a good deal of pleasing ceremony), suddenly stuck at home with nothing to do. I was surrounded by books I could not read, which I occasionally flung across the day nursery in sheer frustration. I was told that my father was away on one of his business trips, though it did seem an abnormally long one. In fact he was in Dachau, having been arrested along with thousands of other Jewish men on Kristallnacht. My mother seemed unusually busy, always out, and provided none of the normal diversions: no stories, no magic-lantern shows, no trips to the shops or the nearby zoo. I took to tiptoeing round the empty front rooms, all unlit. I peered out of the front windows at the street below, busy as usual, streetlamps reflected on wet tarmac and the roofs of passing cars. The Gedächtniskirche already had its Christmas tree, lights sparkling. Why did we not have one? At the other end of the long corridor I could hear whispering: Edith and the nursemaid were discussing some sort of secret. Had my father done something wrong, was he in prison?

———

My nursemaid, tall, blonde and slim, was never very forthcoming at the best of times. She washed and dressed us, did her duty as instructed, but left it at that. No games, no chatter. I had initially resented her arrival, since she replaced the lively dark-haired Käthe, who painted her toe-nails and was heaps of fun. I hope she made it out of Germany.

If the nursemaid did nothing to enliven the hours of tedium while my mother was out of the house, desperately trying to get my father out of Dachau and all the family out of Germany, Edith at least was my friend. When she was not on duty I would visit her in her narrow slip of a room next to the kitchen. It contained an iron bedstead, a small window overlooking the courtyard, and a tiny table display-ing a few personal possessions, which I would examine and ask questions about with the curiosity typical of a small child. Just a few knick-knacks of no particular value except to her, carefully laid out on a white embroidered cloth. She answered my questions patiently, never told me to clear off and leave her in peace.

Edith carrying heaps of clean bedlinen, to be stacked on curtained shelves in the corridor. Edith carrying a large white soup tureen into the main reception room on the rare occasions when we children were permitted to dine at the big table with our parents rather than eating in the day nursery. We sat upright, unusually formal, listening to her footsteps echoing on the bare boards of the long corridor, until the moment when she finally opened the door, carrying a vessel that seemed too large for her, since she was on the short side. We all turned to look at her as she entered and came to the table. I wondered whether the soup could possibly still be hot after such a long trek.

As housemaid, Edith did not do rough work. A fat jolly woman came in daily to clean floors and do the laundry. I would follow her up the back stairs to the attics where tenants could hang washing up to dry and store travel trunks and other clutter. It was a strange, Kafkaesque world of rough partitions and gaps between floorboards which I would – many years later – recognize in *The Trial*.

As for Edith, my most dramatic single memory of her in Berlin occurred a few weeks after my father's disappearance. I suppose I had got used to it by now, my parents' mysterious absence, the fact that I had stopped going to school. It was back to the old routine with my younger brother, which included daily outings with the nursemaid if the weather was fine. And it was fine on that particular morning.

We must have been further afield than usual, possibly shopping, because the three of us were standing on the platform of the tram that conveniently stopped outside our front door, waiting for it to come to a halt. I saw her first: Edith, standing stock-still at the tramstop, obviously to meet

———

us. She wore no coat, although it was winter, just her black and white uniform. I do not know how long she had been standing there, because she seemed to have turned to stone. If she had heard the tram she gave no sign, just continued to stare straight ahead, at nothing in particular. The immobility of some sort of unquestioning obedience.

We got off the tram, spoke to her.

Take the children to their grandparents, she said, as though coming out of her trance. They must not come into the house.

It is my last indelible memory of Edith in Berlin, and the most dramatic. It was the beginning of the end of our life on the Tauenzienstrasse, and from then on no day was quite like any other, and I never knew what tomorrow would bring. Edith standing motionless at the tramstop, like one of those stone statues that mark the entrance to a building of some importance. No. 10 with its imposing portico where the concierge had his little office, its echoing courtyard and sturdy walls rising skyward, was the world as I knew it, and it was starting to fall apart.

Take the children to their grandparents, she had told the nursemaid. They must not come into the house. So half an hour later my brother and I found ourselves in Omi and Opa's three-room apartment on the Bayerischer Platz,

———

———

which did not have a spare bedroom for emergencies. I often played here, and had already settled on the dining-room floor when the telephone rang. My mother, apparently. Yes, everything's fine, replied my grandmother, smiling down at me.

Needless to say, everything was far from fine. My father had been released from Dachau, but was ill with scarlet fever. It would be years before I knew the reasons for my mother's mysterious absences during that bleak November. The endless visits to foreign consulates, the queues of desperate people filling in forms in a manner likely to appease or even hoodwink the Gestapo, a clandestine visit to a member of the Wehrmacht reputed to get prisoners out of concentration camps by bribing the guards. Luckily it was not a trap, and my father was released, though not as promptly as promised. Oh yes, she had also booked a passage by sea to the Far East. We would have taken it if my father had not been too sick to travel.

And where was Edith meanwhile?

I lost sight of her in all this chaos, the daily unexpectedness of everything. My brother and I slept on sofas, which was a bit of a giggle. Then a middle-aged woman arrived to teach us English, for inexplicable reasons. She came about twice, I think, and the little she taught us was so absurd that it makes me laugh to this day, it was so stilted.

The lessons stopped as suddenly as they had started, and

———

we were moved to my other grandmother, who had a vast apartment on the Kurfürstendamm, with plenty of spare bedrooms. Lots of tension here. The nursemaid moved in, and had a shouting match with my duchess of a grand-mother, which fascinated me. Revolution seemed in the air. My mother arrived to pour oil on troubled waters and van-ished as suddenly as she had appeared, without so much as saying hello to me. Life was distinctly odd, grown-ups in particular. I had never seen adults rowing before. The notion of anyone being disrespectful to my stately grand-mother, with her chauffeur-driven Mercedes and large rooms full of old-fashioned furniture, her black silk dresses, her rather dour domestic servants who, like her, seemed unable to get down to a child's level, even to talk, let alone play, was unthinkable. That it was my nursemaid, usually so quiet and withdrawn, was even more surprising.

And then, finally, my brother and I were brought home, and I got the shock of my young life. There had been no warning of any kind, so in my astonishment I paid scant attention to my father. I hardly noticed how thin he was, or that he seemed to have lost most of his hair. The huge reception room, with its dining table at one end and arm-chairs at the other, with a vast, uncluttered Persian carpet lying like an oriental sea between two archipelagos, was almost empty of furniture. A bookcase and bureau remained, but not much else.

My father was watching my wide-eyed reaction with amusement.

Yes, he said, we're going to England.

The abnormality, the falling apart of our lives which had seemed to start with Edith standing sentry in her black and white uniform, was gathering momentum.

The packing that had started during my absence was not over. Large tea-chests appeared on the parquet floor of the living room. Edith and my mother wrapped china and glass, much of it precious. I was told to choose which toys I wanted to take. The doll's house, said my mother, was too big, but I could take the miniature furniture. I picked out my favourite books, and left behind those given to me during my brief, aborted schooldays, unhelpfully printed in the weird German script I would now never learn to read or write, apart from my own name. I seemed to have spent most of my curtailed days at school doing careful pothooks with a dip-pen.

There was a lot of shopping to do. My brother and I were taken to a children's outfitter in our street, Arnold Müller, a rather grand place with a showroom on the first floor. The sort of place where one sat on sofas while ladylike saleswomen brought out their wares. I remember that my brother and I emerged with matching tweed coats, uncomfortably scratchy. Not, I think, that we ever wore them. Perhaps my mother had misjudged the British climate, or else the native styles. In any case, all the clothes brought out of Germany for me to wear became a source of embarrassment. My first classmates in the English elementary school thought I looked weird, and were not backward in saying so.

In normal times my mother often took me out on short shopping trips. To buy fresh fruit or vegetables in the market at the end of the street, on the Wittenbergplatz, for instance. Now she told me I would have to spend my pocket money, which could not be taken to England, and took me into a nearby sweetshop. I think it was on this occasion that she told me that, since we could not take our money with us, we would be very poor once we left Germany. She sounded quite gay about it. Our imminent poverty was impressed on both of us. My four-year-old brother, who was usually left at home on these impromptu shopping trips, had not spent his pocket money. Anxious to help out, he smuggled his few *pfennig*s on to the plane on the day of our departure.

Two altogether more serious and, at the time, more mysterious visits, involving the whole family, are deeply lodged in my memory, even though I did not understand just what

was going on, and why. That the first was of crucial importance was impressed on me by my father on the way. I was
warned to be very good, in a tone of solemnity unusual for
him. We all sat motionless in a grey concrete corridor, not
uttering a word. Further down the corridor I could hear
male voices shouting behind closed doors. The walls seemed
to echo. After what seemed like hours (measured in heart-
beats) we were ushered into a room where a brownshirt,
complete with red armband and high boots, sat on a lofty
podium. It might have been Kafka again, another scene
from *The Trial*. The four of us sat on a bench below. I stared,
my parents sat with their heads bowed. The stormtrooper
shuffled papers about, barked out the odd question, did not
look at us. My father replied in monosyllables. The brownshirt thumped his rubber stamp, and we were let go.

I did not dare ask questions. Emerging from this sinister
building in silence, I turned back at the gate for one last
look. There was a vast grey frontage with many windows on
many floors, all uniformly sized.

We had been given permission to leave this terrifying
country. A considerable sum had to be paid before they
would let us go. We had paid up.

In sharp contrast was the visit to a friendly villa near the
Tiergarten, with the aura of a family home still hanging in

the air. Rows of chairs in the entrance lobby, all of them occupied by silent people. A floor of black and white tiles. From where I was sitting I could look up the broad staircase, to a large window on the landing which let in clear daylight. Nobody went up the stairs, nobody came down them. After a bit we were called into a tiny cubicle of an office under the stairs. A thin man in a grey civilian suit sat behind an unimposing desk. He looked up as the four of us approached the open door, and gave us a friendly smile. I knew he was smiling because of us, the children. I had begun to divide the human race into people who smiled at children, and those who did not. I had begun to study people's faces recently, become much more observant. I was growing up, suddenly and very fast.

Our exit visa had been stamped in the monolithic building where the Gestapo ruled. My father had paid a heavy price, not just in money, for the privilege of leaving the country in which all of us had been born. Now our British visa was being endorsed. It had arrived while my father was ill after Dachau. Otherwise we would have been on that boat to Bangkok.

It is only fair to stress that this visa, precious as it was to people in dire peril, also came with considerable financial conditions attached. Fortunately my parents had money, including a nest-egg which had been accumulating in a British bank. Every Jewish immigrant also had to have a sponsor. In our case it was a Rothschild. Nothing personal, you understand: we came as part of a job lot.

And where was Edith while all this was going on? To be honest, I do not know exactly when she and my nursemaid left our apartment for the last time. I suspect that my mother arranged for them to leave quietly, when we children were out of the way, to avoid tears and unnecessary upsets. There was quite enough heartache in the air. My grandparents showered me with mementoes, bits of jewellery that would outlast my childhood, and a rubber stamp of my name, the name I was born with, in a shiny metal box that has stood the test of time. I have shed the name, but kept the box. For them, always for them.

Sometimes I imagine Edith standing, as she stood that day at the tramstop, watching in the background as we left the building for the last time, but I know it could not have been so. Our heavy front door, with its many locks and bolts, clanged shut on emptiness, on hollow spaces, when it closed behind us for the last time. I remember only my father's nervousness, his haste to be off, and my own distress at the sudden realization that I was losing my grandparents for good. I remember only the two black, chauffeur-driven cars waiting on the pavement, the first with the door open, waiting for us, the second carrying two grandmothers, my grandfather and an aunt. I remember only the cars slowly moving off, and my mother sitting with her head bowed, so she would not, could not see the familiar street slipping away for the last time. It was quite enough for a small child to take in, and remember.

– 3 –

The exodus of German Jews began in 1933, when Hitler came to power. Those who emigrated almost immediately showed foresight, but often not enough. For instance, my father's younger brother Gert settled in London in 1933, while his sister Margot migrated to Paris with her family in the same year. But France was not a good choice, and in 1940 the entire family had to disappear into the Dordogne countryside. They all survived, but the rest of the family were not to know that until the early autumn of 1944, when my father, part of the British Army, was able to visit his sister's Paris apartment and gain the confidence of the concierge, who told him the truth. Others, like Anne Frank's family, left early but chose Holland, with disastrous results.

Many believed that the insanity of the new regime could not possibly last, and hunkered down, waiting for better times. With every passing year the position of the Jews worsened, and so did the international situation. The Nazi rearmament programme was aggressive, and could have only one end. Those who tried to 'get out' dangerously late, particularly after Kristallnacht, when panic set in, knew they had to get as far away as possible. Even England, however desirable, did not seem the safest destination. We arrived in March 1939, but a few days before the declaration of war, in late August, my parents took us to Scotland to stay with acquaintances, convinced that Britain was liable to immediate attack. Fortunately they were wrong, but anyone coming from Germany after witnessing the active preparations for war could be forgiven for having misgivings. Even we children knew that metal was being melted down to make guns, and I experienced my first air-raid siren in the summer of 1938 (just a practice run). The Channel was some defence, but it was not very wide.

The first choice of persecuted Jews in the past had been the US, and it was their first choice now. It was safely out of Hitler's reach. My mother told me in later years that people applying to go to the US would actually fight over the forms that had to be filled in, pieces of paper that promised nothing: for despite the promise of the Statue of Liberty and the country's almost infinite spaces the US had a strict quota system when it came to immigration, ignoring what was clearly becoming a humanitarian emergency. The quotas were based on the ethnic origins of the existing population, so in one sense German Jews were lucky. Many Germans had migrated to America in the nineteenth century and, whatever Hitler might think, a

German Jew was still a German when it came to nationality.

But, given the desperate situation in the late 1930s, the quota was simply inadequate. Some people left Germany for temporary destinations, waiting for their number to come up. Among them were about a thousand people who, having bought visas for Cuba, then hired an ocean liner to take them on a pretend pleasure cruise, but it was really a bid to get out of Germany at any cost. When Cuba refused to honour the visas the ship lay off the US shore for weeks, while the US authorities remained adamant about not allowing the ship to land. Eventually the British government offered to accept a proportion of the passengers, provided that the rest were shared out among other European countries. Of those not lucky enough to get to Britain, very few survived the war. I have met the youngest passenger on that doomed ship, a baby then, with no memory of Germany now. What she does remember is her father letting go of her hand, pushing her away as her parents were arrested. She survived the war through the kindness of French strangers, who brought her up. Ironically, she had an aunt in America, who claimed her after the war, so she lost her adoptive parents too.

Of all the Jews anxious to emigrate from Hitler's Germany, only about 10 per cent considered Palestine an option, despite the considerable inducements offered on both sides, in what amounted to collusion between Nazis and Zionists. The Nazis wanted to get rid of their Jews, and Zionists saw a golden opportunity to get recruits for a cause that had never been popular.

It is not surprising that there were so few applications. German Jews were highly assimilated, and considered themselves Europeans. Many were secular, and intermarriage between Jews and so-called Aryans was very common (a fact that was to cause the regime a few headaches in its attempts to 'purify' the German race). In addition, Germany's Jews were highly urbanized – hardly pioneer material. A great many were educated, had practised as doctors and lawyers or been active in the arts, publishing or retail. (My father's widowed mother lived in considerable luxury in a vast apartment on the Ku'damm, but her sister had married one of the Wertheim brothers, founders of the famous department stores, and that branch of the family was in a different league as far as wealth was concerned. I doubt whether my Wertheim cousins had much difficulty getting into the US, where they still multiply.)

Another deterrent for German Jews when considering Palestine was the fact that they could read. They bought newspapers, and they knew that Palestine was not, as the propaganda adage had it, 'a land without people for a people without land'. On the contrary, there were people living there: Arabs. The well-known writer and journalist Walter Laqueur, who originated from Breslau, explained in his memoir that, having been accepted as a student in Jerusalem, he was entitled to an immigration certificate. In the 'Youth Department' he spoke to an emissary who had gone to Palestine a few years earlier and was now back with a Palestinian passport to act as adviser to young people preparing for life on a kibbutz. (Many Jewish educational establishments were training their pupils for a life on the land, not in a city.) Walter Laqueur asked him about the fighting in Palestine – German papers were full of reports of Arab insurgents taking over the country. He was told that the reports were exaggerated and that in any case Arabs were no match for the British, or even the Jews.

Laqueur's experience of Jerusalem in 1938 was, as he himself put it, not 'uplifting'. It looked and smelled like an oriental city: small houses, often derelict, dusty streets full of merchants advertising their wares, and donkeys braying. There were open spaces between houses where rubbish had been dumped, very few trees and no grass. Jerusalem was divided by ethnic origin – Arabs in the old city, neighbourhoods of Orthodox Jews, and districts where Jews from oriental countries lived. Rehavia, on the other hand, was a middle-class garden suburb mainly inhabited by German Jews. They had small gardens and lots of trees.

—————

They often owned a grand piano, read Goethe and played Schubert.

In all, it was a population that had come from all over the world, with a bewildering variety of languages, clothes and customs. But however much the various groups might dislike and distrust each other, they all united in hating the *yekke*s, as Jews from Germany were called. After 1933 they were often called 'Hitler Zionists', people who had merely come to save their own skins, not out of deep Zionist conviction. Some of them even wanted to establish friendly relations with the Arabs, which went against every Zionist instinct.

Many of these 'Hitler Zionists', including Laqueur, left Palestine as soon as it was safe to do so, after the defeat of Germany in 1945.

Hitler's rise to power was a golden opportunity for Zionists to promote their cause. They had always prospered during pogroms, but this one was unique, unprecedented. For a long time Germany had been seen as the land of opportunity for the poor Jews of eastern Europe, and those who had settled there had prospered, done rather too well for a country now going through hard times, with the perhaps inevitable backlash. The Jews provided a convenient scapegoat.

—————

———

There was one significant difference between this wave of potential immigrants to Palestine and previous *aliyah*s. Unlike previous immigrants from the east, German Jews had money and property, which could help the Zionist cause. The idea of making a pact with the Devil did not take long to burgeon, even though some Jewish settlers were uneasy about doing business with the Nazis. But business they certainly did.

The result was the Haavara (or 'transfer') Agreement, and negotiations started early in 1933. Though details of the agreement were adjusted from time to time, in the main the Haavara operated through trust companies set up in Germany and Palestine. Before leaving Germany the Jewish emigrants deposited their capital with the German trust company, which used the money to pay German suppliers for merchandise meant for export to Palestine. The people in Palestine who ordered merchandise from Germany transferred their payments to a local trust company, who returned the money to the Jews who had meanwhile arrived from Germany. It was a complex system but it benefited all those involved. The Nazis got rid of some of their Jews and also got round international boycotts. The Zionist movement acquired new settlers, who in turn escaped from Germany with more capital than they might otherwise have done.

The system continued to function until the middle of the

———

Second World War, and was always controversial. Some 20,000 people were helped by this scheme, and about $30,000 transferred from Germany to Palestine. The immigrants themselves had to wait a long time for their money, and lost about 35 per cent of it. The *yekkes* might be disliked for their superior attitudes and distaste for aggressive nationalism, of which they had seen quite enough in their homeland, but the money they brought helped the Zionist cause, which had often been dependent on the charity of wealthy European Jews.

After the Anschluss Eichmann was made responsible for getting rid of Austria's Jews. He went so far as to visit Palestine, then warmly recommended it to departing Jews, while extorting their 5,000 Reichsmarks, the sum required for an exit visa.

Despite the Haavara, and despite the increasingly desperate plight of Europe's Jews, the Zionists did not want just anyone to come to Palestine. They wanted the young, fit and strong. Life was hard, and physical fitness was required. On occasion they would complain about the 'material' being sent to them. They could not afford to look after the sick and elderly. Three years after the Nazis came to power, and with a world war clearly on the horizon, a special fund was established in Palestine to finance the return of incurably ill Jews to Europe, on the grounds that these immigrants had become a burden on the community. By the end of 1936 this fund had made arrangements for the return of several dozen immigrants.

Zionists and Nazis had more in common than is generally acknowledged.

What has been called the 'second diaspora' more or less came to an end with the outbreak of war in September 1939, though a small trickle of Jews managed to leave Germany until 1941, when the Nazis put an end to any further emigration. Some ended up in South America, others in the Far East. Shanghai was known to be the one destination that required no entry visa, but it was not a popular one.

So who was left when this exodus came to an end? In the main it was the poor, the elderly and single women, because they were unlikely to be self-supporting, which made them unacceptable to countries willing to take refugees. Edith was poor and single. Oddly enough Britain, suffering an acute shortage of domestic servants, did admit single women on domestic permits, but most of the women who got in under this guise seem to have been middle-class. My father's elder sister was one of them.

Aunt Lotte was a lovable eccentric who had eschewed marriage to devote herself to music and painting. She lived in my grandmother's vast apartment, and when my brother and I had to stay there while my father was sick after his stay in Dachau she had also taken up photography. One room had been turned into a studio, where she took very posed portraits of me and my brother. I am wearing my best dress, cradling my favourite doll. My hair is unnaturally smooth and tidy.

Anyhow, at the last possible moment Lotte decided to join her siblings in London, and arrived in the summer of 1939. True to form, her luggage got left behind, but I remember the family reunion as a moment of great joy: June, bright sunshine, all of us laughing and otherwise speechless. Lottchen had a wonderful laugh and, best of all, she was able to laugh at herself when the rest of us found her behaviour amusing, which happened not infrequently, given her eccentricity. The fact that Lottchen had entered the UK on a domestic permit, having never so much as made her own bed or boiled an egg, was a source of some hilarity. She found herself a bedsit in Oxford, having decided that only there was the intellectual tone up to her level, and got through the war by giving piano lessons. On her frequent visits to us in London she almost invariably had to go back to Paddington because her suitcase had been left behind.

People like Edith, on the other hand, had neither the know-how nor the wherewithal to get out of Germany. I doubt whether the possibility even occurred to her. She

———

knew how to fetch and carry, obey simple instructions, but was barely literate. There were no books in her narrow room in the Tauenzienstrasse, not even cheap romances or thrillers, and I never saw her read a newspaper. People like her, brought up in an orphanage in the first decades of the twentieth century, would not have been offered much in the way of education other than the three Rs. Her future in service was pretty much predestined.

Unlike my Aunt Lotte, Edith was expected to make her own bed almost as soon as she could walk. By the time she left the institution she knew how to boil an egg without cracking it, prepare vegetables for cooking, iron shirts and blouses without scorching, that sort of thing. She might not earn much, but she would always have a roof over her head. At a time of great economic uncertainty there still seemed to be enough people in Berlin whose savings had not been wiped out by the hyperinflation and who still regarded a live-in servant as a necessity. My father's mother was one such person. Her money was invested in property, and my father remembered having to collect tenants' rents on a daily basis as rents, like the cost of everything else, went up almost by the hour. My mother spent her first wages, earned by working in a theatrical design studio, on anything she could buy in a hurry. Like most daughters of the period, she lived at home with her parents until she married my father.

*

———

———

By the standards and expectations of the time, before 1933, Edith had all the skills she needed to survive. No one could know, as she faced the world on leaving the orphanage, that she would require so much more to survive the years ahead.

———

When, almost a decade after I had last seen her, Edith
decided to try and join us in London, what did she imagine
she would find? I doubt whether she gave the matter much
thought. Lonely, rootless and unhappy, I think she was overwhelmed by a nostalgia for the past, the last time she felt
content and secure, part of a family who had treated her
well.

What was that family in the top-floor apartment of the
Tauenzienstrasse really like? They were young, good-
natured and, by the standards of the period, informal. My
father was an extrovert who adored playing with his children, romping about. Completely untrained as a musician,
he loved to sing, anything from Schubert to the latest pop
song, and would occasionally play his Hohner mouth organ,
if only to teach us how to master our own. He acquired a
piano accordion at one point, presumably to go with the
yacht moored on the Havel, though it disappeared from
sight as quickly as it had made its first appearance in the
apartment. Herr Unger was often away on business, as
trade representative of various prestigious British textile

firms. When he was at home Edith was busier, particularly
in the kitchen. My father liked his food, was something of a
martinet when it came to meals, and my mother saw it as
her most important duty as his wife to serve up his favourite
food, cooked to perfection. So she always took charge of the
kitchen, with Edith and the daily woman merely helping
out, scouring pans, fetching and carrying.

My mother was much quieter than my father. Inhibited,
I think now. She took no part in the Sunday-morning romps
in the master bedroom, merely watching quietly, a faint
smile on her face. At bedtime my father would sing from a
large illustrated songbook while I studied the pictures and
tried to join in. If it was my mother's turn she would read
stories. The favourite for both of us was about a cute little
girl and her antics, published in 1906 and obviously dating
back to her own childhood. Of course there were other stories – Hans Christian Andersen, Pinocchio – but sooner or
later it was back to Appelschnut, whose real name was
Roswitha.

Unlike my father, she was not physical. I do not recall
getting a good-night kiss from her. My father, on the other
hand, would pretend to be a tiger trying to eat me up, and
send me into shrieks of giggles. Not only did my mother
not give cuddles, she was also obsessed with hygiene. The
night nursery had to be a germ-free zone, and she always
wore a white overall when she entered it. Whenever I was

ill, then or later, she was like a conscientious nurse. The
room was aired, food, drink and medication scrupulously
administered at the correct times and in the right doses.
What she never did, then or later, was to come in and just
keep me company for a bit. So I remember the woodwork,
painted white, the wallpaper with red roses running diagon-
ally up to the ceiling. I remember the green blind flapping,
its acorn toggle at the end of a string which I could just
reach from my cot when I could not sleep after lunch. But
most of all I remember listening to my mother's footsteps
treading the long corridor on the far side of the door with
its frosted-glass panels, hoping against hope that she would
come in.

She must have been a good employer in those days, or
Edith would not have wanted to come back so many years
later. In fact I am sure she was. I never heard her raise her
voice in anger, or lose patience. And one image sticks in my
mind to suggest that Edith was right to feel herself part of
the family. On the only festive Christmas I remember, which
must have been in 1937, I recall seeing my mother handing
a gift to Edith from the big table beside the tree. It was very
much a family occasion. My grandmother from the
Ku'damm was there; so was my Uncle Gert, who had come
over from England. The fact that Edith joined in the festiv-
ities shows that she regarded herself as part of the family.
And that my mother probably realized she had nowhere

else to go. My nursemaid, on the other hand, had stuck around long enough to get her two charges dressed up for the evening but had later disappeared.

I sometimes wonder what sort of person I would have become if history had not taken such an abnormal turn, if I had grown up in Berlin, well-to-do, privileged. I have occasionally passed half an hour in some café in Charlottenburg, watching the traffic go by and wondering. There is no obvious answer. I expect I would have found some way of rebelling against the family norms, the expectations of my class. Whether I would have become a writer is a somewhat problematic question, since I think the sudden change of language at an early age did more than anything else to excite me in that direction. There was one particular moment in the autumn of 1940 when a teacher spoke to me in English and I suddenly realized that I had understood what was being said to me, *all of it*. It began a passionate fascination with language that has never left me.

It is also impossible to say whether the war and its losses affected me more deeply than other people. I know that seeing the newsreels of Belsen in April 1945 changed me for ever, and that I was not the same person afterwards. Because the event coincided with my first period, I have always associated that visit to the Odeon cinema with the menarche, my change from childhood to womanhood. An unfortunate association, since from then on I would always equate my menstrual cycle with a recurring wound doomed never to heal.

On the surface I was fairly normal for my age. I went mad on the New Look and outraged members of the school staff by coming to school in an ankle-length skirt. Britain did not have teenagers in those days, and when an American pen-friend sent me bright red lipstick with matching nail varnish my father was horrified – it was only fit for tarts, possibly girlfriends, but not wives and daughters, he told me firmly. I was, explained my mother, a *Backfisch*, neither fish nor flesh, child or woman, but something in between. So my first lipstick, purchased by her, was palest pink.

But that was all on the surface. After years of austerity, fashion was suddenly fun. But what I had seen in the Odeon cinema on that April afternoon meant my entire view of the world had changed for ever. It was not only the personal loss. My opinion of the human race had changed radically.

My father once said I reminded him of a sister who had committed suicide years before I was born. I was inclined to 'take things too seriously'. Perhaps it was just adolescent self-consciousness, but I thought other people also noticed

---

it. When I looked in the mirror I saw it reflected in the solemnity of my dark eyes. I thought other people saw it too, and that they turned away in embarrassment.

My school reports do suggest such a divide. In the lower school I got reprimands for being a chatterbox, for not always paying attention in class. Further up the school I revelled in my ability to write English essays in any style, often insincere, and still get top marks. I did most of my learning at the public library, where I worked my way methodically through the adult shelves, unaware that I was supposed to be confining myself to the children's section. At school I frequently had a book open under the desk when the lesson bored me.

But underneath the breezy confidence was a girl, neither fish nor flesh, with a wound that would not heal. It enabled me to understand why Edith had come back to us, when she did finally arrive.

I have been told that men are less deeply affected by the trauma of displacement and loss. It is certainly an interesting theory, but as far as my brother was concerned, I think he was simply too young. By the time he started school at the age of five in September 1939 he was thoroughly assimilated, spoke English like a native, and could drop his aitches with the best of them. He was rather too good at becoming one of the lads, so, with my father back home from the army, he became a day-boy at Highgate School. My mother wanted

---

him back in the social class to which he rightly belonged, and to become a doctor if possible. The English public schoolboy greeted Edith with his old, dimpled smile, but spoke hardly any German.

As for my father, he had probably changed least of all. The fact that he spent the war in the Pioneer Corps, made up of other refugees from Germany and Austria, meant that he was curiously isolated from the everyday realities of British life. The men spoke German when they were off duty, and played German card games. It was a source of considerable amusement to the family that, having started off as the only member of the family with a modicum of English, he was now woefully backward. So Herr Unger was much the same. Housemaids, in any case, were not his sphere. That was women's stuff. It was my mother who had changed most of all, in ways that were not obvious to those outside the immediate family circle. Having re-entered it, Edith would discover this to her cost.

To all outward appearances, it was a good time in our lives. It was a time of reconstruction, of hope. Still an era of austerity, yes, but also of optimism, of freedom from fear. Pleasures that someone of my generation could only dream about were suddenly a possibility. Going abroad for a holiday, even though the currency restrictions were severe. West

———

End theatres opening up, with jolly American musicals about corn in Kansas lighting up the grey world of post-war London. The glitter and splendour of Covent Garden on special occasions – Margot Fonteyn dancing Cinderella on my birthday, for example. War films went out of fashion and the New Look came in, making women suddenly ultra-feminine again. Not since the First World War and female emancipation had the skirts been so long and full, waists so tiny. You could even buy shampoo to wash your hair on a Friday night, instead of using soapflakes.

When my mother decided to go to art school as a girl, her father had made her learn dressmaking too, as a standby occupation. This had been very useful during the war, when she found herself in great demand, adapting dresses or cutting garments out of a spare length of material. Neighbours would often pop in for a fitting, and she seemed to spend half her life with pins in her mouth, adjusting hems. Luckily an electric sewing machine had come with us from Germany. She not only helped out the neighbours, but she seemed to take genuine pleasure in turning the rebellious, often difficult child of the war years into a clothes-conscious young woman who, despite the rationing, always had a party dress to wear for the end-of-term dance. I must admit I was not always grateful, finding fault, the way girls do. I also learnt to sew things for myself, with my mother only finishing off the difficult bits.

———

———

I think she was partly motivated by the fact that, despite my bookishness, I was turning out to be normal after all. My mother's great fear, I was to discover a few years later, was that I might end up an eccentric, like my Aunt Lotte, and not do what girls were supposed to do in the fullness of time: get married and start a family.

The truth is, my mother and I had had our own private war between 1939 and 1945. With my father away in the Pioneer Corps, and my brother eventually sent off to a boarding school in Hampshire because my mother could not 'handle' him without a man around, I spent most of the war, apart from a blissful year of evacuation, alone with my mother in a small suburban flat in Kingsbury, north London. She became first depressed, then increasingly resentful of the whole situation, and she took it out on me, one way and another, because there was nobody else around. Now and then she would blame my father for going off and leaving her to cope with everything on her own. Mostly she blamed me for being a nuisance, not helping out enough, not cleaning enough floors, not washing more dishes. 'I don't like your attitude,' she would say when, having failed to please her, I became sulky and unresponsive.

My father's weekend leaves, before he was sent to

———

———

Normandy, were invariably spoilt (for both of us) by a litany of complaints about my behaviour. I could hear them talking in the bedroom, and then my poor father would emerge and give me a lecture on being helpful to my mother. I protested that I was trying, and it was the truth. I took to buying her presents with my pocket money and, when that ran out, with money stolen from the bureau. Nothing helped. Unable to win her love, I think I ended up hating her. I think we ended up hating each other. If we sat opposite each other we would exchange a cold stare. 'I don't expect you to love me,' she once announced, 'but I do expect respect.' A remark which I found contemptible.

At this distance in time it is possible to be dispassionate about the situation, to pity her rather than myself. Unfortunately those war years would mar our relationship for the rest of her life, particularly after my father's death many years later, when her old hostility, possibly sharpened by guilt, resurfaced. My father, who was to have his own difficulties with her in the post-war years, always maintained that we owed our lives to her, that she had done everything to get us out of Germany, pulled all the strings, greased the right palms, filled in the necessary forms in the necessary fashion, omitting information detrimental to our case, such as the British bank account. I found such initiative hard to credit, knowing her as I did. Someone who,

———

as my uncle once said, behaved throughout the war as though Hitler had been invented specifically to make her life unpleasant. Someone who, as I remember, was always moaning on about something: the rationing, the air raids, my father's selfish and inconsiderate absence, and, as the person nearest to hand, my behaviour, which was invariably at fault. I did not speak when spoken to, or worse, answered back. I did my homework instead of doing the housework – not just some of it, but all of it. Bad news from abroad was used as a weapon to hit me with, including my grandparents' deportation in 1942, when I was just ten years old.

When the camps were opened up three years later she sent me on my own to watch the newsreel of horrors showing at the Hendon Odeon. I was so used to her treatment of me by that time that this struck me as perfectly normal until years later, when other people expressed their horror. 'Go and see what they have done,' she said that afternoon in April, in a tone of fury which felt as though it was directed at me personally. When I got back neither of us spoke for the rest of the day, reduced to a silence destined to last for years.

Looking back, I have come to the conclusion that my mother was good at dealing with an immediate crisis, whether it was a sick child or my father in Dachau, but could not cope with the long haul, the unending tedium of a long war, what was referred to as 'the duration'. Come to think of it, we did have our good moments: going to the cinema. Sheer escapism. And it brought us together for a bit. I would prolong the fun by mimicking the best bits for several days. Anton Walbrook was our favourite: he looked like my father and went in for roles that required a foreign accent, Prince Albert for example, and the Polish concert pianist in *Dangerous Moonlight*.

On the home front 'the duration' required endurance rather than courage. Sleepless nights, getting reluctant children out of bed when the siren wailed, making tea for the neighbours when the all-clear sounded. Food-rationing meant an endless challenge to the housewife. I know I tended to complain when I was sent up the road to the fish and chip shop for the third time in a week. With a dish, since my mother did not believe in the flavour-enhancing properties of newspaper. As 'enemy aliens', despite my father's khaki uniform, any travel out of London involved reporting to the police, a particular grievance with my mother, and for once I think she had a point.

Daylight raids in 1940 were followed by night raids, which in turn were followed by doodlebugs, the flying bombs. At least you could see them coming and take cover. These were followed by supersonic rockets, the most terrifying of all, since there was no prior warning. Everyone was tired, everyone left in London had lost their nerve. The end might be in sight by the summer of 1944, but it did not feel like it. My grammar school stayed shut for weeks on end, in the interests of safety. We just came in for homework once a fortnight. Almost everyone in our block of flats had left for the country, so the neighbourhood felt ghostly. 'Holidays at home' was government policy, amounting to the odd funfair and a conjuror in the local park. My mother and a neighbour clubbed together to take me and her younger son to Brighton for a week, but the beach was covered in landmines and barbed wire, and flying bombs passed overhead on their way to London.

At last came D-Day, a hot day in early June, with all windows open and every wireless blaring the latest news into the street. Our geography lessons were now dominated by Normandy, as we followed the Allied progress inch by inch on our maps. Not till the autumn did the momentum seem unstoppable. 'All over by Christmas'? If Churchill and Montgomery had had their way it might well have been. But Eisenhower was Commander-in-Chief now and he had other ideas. He went south, instead of making a run for Berlin, as agreed between Roosevelt and Stalin at Yalta. To Stalin's amazement the Americans actually stuck to the deal, something he himself was not in the habit of doing. So the war was won but the peace lost, at least as far as half of Europe was concerned. Poland, for which Britain had gone

———

to war in the first place, was still not free, just under a different tyranny.

The young and innocent might celebrate VE Day. I did, though conscious of loss. Others did not. My mother went to bed early and lay awake, staring at the ceiling.

———

$$- 5 -$$

By 1948 the war really was over, at least superficially. In other ways it would never be over. The missing waved good-bye in my dreams, standing at the edge of Tempelhof airfield, and faded at dawn. But here we were, with the nuclear family at least restored to normality, living together under the same roof. My father turned forty shortly after driving his army lorry on to the Normandy beaches, so he was demobbed fairly early on. He was once more the breadwinner, his authority as head of the family for the most part undisputed. His attitudes were undoubtedly patriarchal, but I was happy to let him have his way, at least for the moment. I knew the rules, and as long as I obeyed them I felt relatively safe from the explosions of emotional and physical abuse I had suffered during his absence. Hearing his shocked rebuke to my mother when she smacked my face in public was a landmark in itself. The crockery stopped flying. I had once pleaded to a friendly neighbour for help, telling her that my mother 'had gone mad', and been laughed at for my pains. Now I had protection.

But the small suburban flat really would not do, particularly

----

if my brother was to come back to London from his Hampshire prep school. Apart from anything else, my father found it embarrassing to have an adolescent daughter around. I learnt to stay out of the way when he was using the bathroom.

So in the famously bitter winter of 1947 we moved into the four-bedroomed semi-detached house in Hendon, and for the first time in my life, at the age of fifteen, I had a room of my own, my own private space. After the gipsy-like existence of the war years, sleeping in makeshift accommodation, whether in London or elsewhere, in my brother's room if he was away at school, on the sofa in the dining room if he was home, I was in seventh heaven. As far as I was concerned it was the best room in the house, since it overlooked the garden, and was slightly bigger than my parents' room. Up to a point I was even allowed to choose my own decoration. White was considered too extreme in the 1940s but I was allowed cream paintwork and pale beige and white striped wallpaper. Apart from a new 'utility' bed, new furniture was out of the question in those austerity days, but a desk and chair that had belonged to my uncle's new wife were sprayed white for my use.

This was my kingdom, my retreat. Shelves were put up for my books, and on my next birthday I even got a small bakelite wireless, also cream-coloured. I got a thrill every time I entered my private kingdom, and left it only with reluctance.

Under my father's relatively benevolent but nevertheless patriarchal reign I was required to leave my sanctuary all too often. I was forever at my mother's beck and call, though the chores she wanted done were far less arduous than they had been. I think her main objective was not to leave me in peace at any price. So I was constantly being asked to set the table for lunch, shell peas, dry dishes: whatever. Feeling it was a small price to pay for everything I now enjoyed, I would – if the silence went on too long – offer my services, call out 'Can I do anything?' My mother could always be relied upon to think of something. If all else failed I would be asked to clean the bathroom washbasin, a chore I have disliked ever since as a result.

My brother, being a boy, and now attending an expensive school in the hopes that he would become a doctor, a very Jewish-mother's ambition he nevertheless failed to fulfil, was excused from all domestic chores on account of his gender. In any case, he was ensconced in the attic, happily out of earshot, usually pestering unseen birds with his airgun. My own requirement to help in the house, which climaxed in my having to cook Sunday lunch, was also supposed to be educational. I was learning to be a good housewife, as society, as far as my mother was concerned, required of me.

What was to be Edith's room still stood empty, but a cleaner now came regularly, so that I only had to be available for light duties, what was considered suitable for the daughter of the house in middle-class homes. Middling middle, so to speak. I had not seen the house before we moved in, and my mother made it clear to me that it was 'the best we can afford'. In other words, not up to the standard she had once been used to. But the fourth bedroom in the attic, plus a system of bell-pushes in the main rooms, which no longer worked, and an indicator panel in the kitchen to show the room number, made it clear that the original occupants had had a live-in maid. Lifeless though it was, or perhaps because it never did anything, that panel had a sort of fascination for me. As though it was trying to tell me something. Why this anachronism?

Certainly family life became markedly more formal after we moved into the Hendon house. Mealtimes were a bit of a trial, with a certain amount of parental bickering, now that normal married life had been resumed. My father was always served first, and his verdict on the food was awaited with bated breath. His approval usually meant a relatively relaxed occasion. Weekends usually meant rather more protracted entertainment, often formal luncheons with guests eating from the best china and staying on for tea. A tea trolley was acquired, a patio built. I never quite knew when it was safe to slip away to the sanctuary of my room.

I never knew just how much money my parents had managed to squirrel away in a British bank account to finance our flight from Germany, but it seems to have been enough, not just for the house in Hendon, but for something even more urgent, once the war was over. So in the summer of 1946 we took a trip to Switzerland, 'to eat', my mother said. For years she had been telling me of such pre-war delights as profiteroles and omelettes. Now it was time, to put it crudely, to stuff ourselves silly. The delights would start, I was promised, when we changed trains at the border between France and Switzerland. In Basle, she said, we would breakfast on white rolls and black cherry jam. She was as good as her word.

We had entered a sort of fairyland, where one could get anything. Just anything.

I had vague memories of the hotel high above Lake Lucerne because I had been there at the age of three. It had been a family reunion of sorts: my mother, my Aunt Margot from Paris with her two boys, and my grandmother, who probably footed the bill. The underlying reason for holding such a family reunion outside Germany is only clear to me now. By 1935 Jews were not welcome in most German hotels. The few holidays I can remember prior to 1939 were all taken abroad, usually to ski. In summer we had the weekend house, and sailed on the Havel.

In 1946, coming from a country with severe rationing, I

was very conscious of my wardrobe, or rather my lack of it. We had to change for dinner, and I found myself alternating between two cotton frocks hanging forlornly in the middle of a vast wardrobe. I felt like a poor relation of some sort. In Lucerne I could not get over the sheer luxury of everything, houses freshly painted, shops bursting with books and stationery, both hard to come by in England. To say nothing of the food. At café tables, where we ordered iced coffees and meringues with whipped cream, I marvelled at the presence of paper napkins, wrapped sugar cubes, drinking straws, and whirls of butter on ice.

On the way home I saw Paris for the first time, and got reacquainted with my aunt and two cousins. In those days Paris enjoyed an almost legendary status as the centre of glamour and sophistication, which had perhaps been heightened by the fact that it had been beyond reach all through the war. 'That's Paris,' said my mother, in a tone of almost religious awe, as the train approached the city lights under a night sky. What I saw in daylight was far from glamorous. If anything the city was shabbier than London, somehow antiquated, its traffic chaotic, smelly and unhygienic. No bombsites, but otherwise a raddled old woman who had run out of make-up and perfume.

So perhaps I was not such a poor relation after all? My elder cousin, who had been in the Resistance during the war, liked to tease me about Joan of Arc, whereupon I would get my own back by mentioning Winston Churchill and the French collapse of 1940. Now, seeing the white cliffs of Dover on our return, and presenting my brand-new British passport, I felt proud, patriotic too. No less a person than His Majesty's Principal Secretary of State for Foreign Affairs, Ernest Bevin, did request and require that I should be allowed to 'pass freely and without let or hindrance' and should be afforded 'every assistance and protection of which she may stand in need'.

I knew who I was, and where I belonged. There were bluebirds over the white cliffs of Dover that afternoon.

———

– 6 –

When Edith wrote from Palestine, the newly created Israel, asking for her old job back, I was both incredulous and excited. My mother wrote back telling her to come, and her imminent arrival was constantly on my mind during the intervening weeks.

Edith was not my grandmother, I did not grieve for her during the recurring dream of leaving. She had not been at the airport to wave goodbye. So far as I could remember she had not even said goodbye. Nevertheless she was part of the emotional landscape of long ago, now eradicated by death and ruin. Her footfalls echoed down the long uncarpeted corridor between kitchen and public reception rooms, past the day nursery and the night nursery and my parents' bedroom. I could reconstruct every room and every item of furniture in that apartment, including her narrow slip of a room, even though I knew that the entire building had been turned to rubble by the RAF or American bombers. I knew this from the aerial photographs that appeared in the *News Chronicle*, and had it confirmed after the war because the building formed part of my grandmother's estate. I had heard them myself, the steady drone of bombers leaving for Germany night after night, and they had been as sooth-ing as a lullaby. Your turn now, I would think, before dozing off, sure in my own mind that nobody I cared about was by now left alive in Berlin.

I was wrong. Not just Edith, but my grandmother was being hidden by Germans when the unrelenting bombing began. My father's mother bought her way out of Germany to Sweden in the summer of 1944, only to die in her bed a few months later. Edith, without a penny to her name, sur-vived not only the round-up of Jews and the carpet-bombing of Berlin but also the final battle, fought street by shattered street, when Russian troops reached the city.

A far as I was concerned, Edith was family, and I knew instinctively that this was her reason for seeking us out after such a long time, and from so far away. So it was with a growing sense of unease that I began to realize that my mother did not know this or, if she did, thought it of no consequence. Since the end of the war her main aim in life had been reconstruction, to get back the lifestyle, as nearly as possible, she had enjoyed before Hitler had ruined every-thing. Edith's return could not have been more timely: she had the house, she had the small spare room, now she would have the housemaid to put in it.

It is as though she had learnt nothing from the cata-strophe that had overwhelmed the world. My mother's entire existence, after 1945, was focused on social status, on keeping up appearances, on being slightly better, in terms of material possessions, than her neighbours and other people she knew. A childhood friend, son of our family doctor during the war years, remembers her as 'very genteel'. He was astonished when I recently told him about what went on behind closed doors, her violent temper, the physical and verbal abuse I was regularly subjected to.

Perhaps it should be put down to an underlying inse-curity, a lack of self-worth, which had to be compensated for by material possessions and a ladylike presence. My 'cleverness' certainly riled her. As Ruth, my uncle's wife, put it years later: 'She was very proud of you, until you began to know more than she did.' If I tried to help with her English, for instance, she took it the wrong way, as an offence to her dignity. My parents had married when she was pregnant with me, normal enough in those days of unreliable birth control, but she tried to hide the fact all her life by falsifying dates in albums and other memen-toes, and by celebrating their silver wedding a year early. And because of her pregnancy, and some joke my father had made at the time about making sure his future wife was fertile, she was never quite sure that he had married her for the 'right' reasons. She never forgot what he had

---

———

said, never forgave him, and was partly unsure of him for ever.

Since we had been able to bring out material possessions from the Berlin apartment, post-war life in the newly acquired house enabled her to show off expensive furniture and other things. Hopelessly large for the two wartime flats we occupied, some of the oriental carpets had been sold off, and even now it was necessary to cut the backs off bulkier items, the sideboard for example. No rooms would ever be as spacious as those we had occupied in Berlin. But once we had settled in, spent all our coupons on floor-length curtains, enhanced the phoney Tudor look with phoney Tudor antiques to go with the false beams and English brick fireplace, she was able to display the cut glass, the monogrammed cutlery and above all the best porcelain, made – as she never tired of telling me – in the royal factory founded by Frederick the Great. There was stacks of the stuff, a large dinner service and a matching set for coffee or tea.

My mother came into her own if guests were expected for Sunday lunch. She was always immensely pleased with herself when I helped her to put an extra leaf into the heavy dining table and spread out the starched white tablecloth of finest damask. She was, I think, truly happy at such moments. The food was also good on such occasions. Ingredients were easier to get and she had brought out her

———

———

voluminous German cook book, her bible for married life in the old days.

It was, in her mind, almost like old times. Perhaps she was able to fool herself into thinking that the old days really were back, and what had happened in the interim could be forgotten, as though it had never been. Except that she was no longer the gentle, rather reserved young woman of the 1930s, who had in fact married rather 'above' her own status into a family of stupendous wealth, and who was therefore in no position to show off, and probably did not want to.

Things were different now. My grandmother was dead, the Wertheims had settled in America, and we had, to my great relief, declined an invitation to join them in a chicken-farming venture. Our immediate family had shrunk, and our most frequent Sunday guests were my Uncle Gert and Ruth, his new second wife. My uncle was charming but feckless, apparently borrowed money he did not return, and was suspected of having taken the very large diamond on his wife's engagement finger from my grandmother's safe-deposit box in Berlin – a factor, perhaps, in the rather nasty, spiteful pride my mother always took in being better off than them. She sneered when they bought a house in Hampstead because it was small and awkwardly designed, conveniently ignoring the fact that Hampstead was a far more desirable address. Years later, when both couples had

———

moved out of London, she was forever gloating over the fact that her garden was bigger. It was not enough for her to enjoy returning good fortune: it had to be at somebody else's expense.

People are not really changed by events; they develop in what is probably a pre-ordained way, according to circumstances. She did not make my father happy in the post-war years, and he walked out on her once, for a brief period. He also expressed his feeling of guilt at having left me to her untender mercies during the war. Being incapable of showing love, she could not give way to grief either, only anger. Over the years she developed a pathological hatred of her stepmother, my beloved Omi, blaming her for her father's death in the gas chamber. The fact that my grandmother had also died did not concern her. Any mention of her invariably resulted in an outburst of rage.

My own perspective was very different. I had grown up in a world of hardship and shortages. I was cleaning floors at the age of ten, earning a minuscule amount of pocket money in return. Nobody I knew had a live-in servant. Those days were over, and quite right too. Although still far too young to vote in 1945, I had been thrilled by the Labour landslide, jumping up and down with excitement as the results came in on the school library wireless, where I and a few other students had been invited to listen in by a new young English teacher, born too late to go and fight.

As for Edith, she was a special case.

In the weeks before she was due to arrive I would, on my return from school, often peep into the spare room to see how the preparations were going. I expected to see a few welcoming touches in what had been a very bare space: a few cushions perhaps, a nice mirror to make up for the lack of a dressing table, maybe a vase on the windowsill. But only one new item appeared in the room, a spartan washstand. The black metal frame held a white enamel bowl with a matching jug underneath.

I was shocked. The washstand made a clear statement: Edith was to take her ablutions separately; even though she would sleep on our landing, she would not take her turn in the bathroom like the rest of us. Admittedly taking turns in the bathroom, especially first thing in the morning, required speed and an unspoken rota, but was absolutely normal by the standards of the time. During the worst of the Blitz I had spent a year in a small boarding school, where three members of staff and up to a dozen children took turns in the only bathroom, the latter being bathed in twos and threes. I had been an evacuee in various households, including an old farmhouse without electricity. I had stayed in boarding houses with fancy china bowls and matching jugs, and a proper bathroom down the hall. I had been temporarily billeted with a variety of strangers. And never in all those years had I come across such an unfriendly object, let alone been required to use it. To me it spoke of a bygone age, the Dickensian world familiar from my favourite reading. It had no place in the brave new world which had come into being with the recent election.

I did not know what to do. Knowing my mother, I did nothing.

And then she was suddenly there, when I got home from school one afternoon. At first it struck me how little she had changed, as she stood in the dining room talking to my mother, then turned to look at me. Her skin was a little rougher perhaps, and there were a few streaks of grey in her coarse black hair, but otherwise she was still the same old Edith. As far as I was concerned the only surprise was seeing her out of uniform, in clothes clearly intended for English weather: a beige woollen sweater and a tartan skirt in darker shades of brown. At least, in the days that followed, my mother made no attempt to get her kitted out in a traditional housemaid's uniform. Whether she considered it I do not know. Perhaps too many clothing coupons had gone on the chintz curtains, or possibly she had made enquiries in Golders Green, but without success. 'No call for them, madam' she would have been told, in the tone commonly adopted by the salesladies of 1948.

TWO

The arrival of Edith meant news from across the chasm of death. What, for instance, had happened to Schwester Eva? I caught my mother whispering the question either on that first afternoon or very shortly afterwards. What was significant was the whisper, even though there was nobody else in the room, until I happened to walk in. That was how things were in those days: nobody spoke of such things out loud, if at all. Silence was the norm for years on end.

After Edith left the room my mother told me that my Berlin nursemaid had died of typhus in one of the camps. She then went on to speculate that she had probably been spared the gas chamber because she was a *Mischling*, of mixed race. I doubt whether this fact had anything to do with the manner of her dying, since thousands of Jews died of disease, especially in the last months of the war. But I began to see her differently from then on, the quiet slender blonde who did her duty but no more. Dark-haired, stocky little Edith had managed to survive, while her workmate had gone quietly to her death. I was sure of it, that she had obediently packed her small suitcase and reported at the assembly point as ordered. It fitted in with the young woman I remembered. I never saw her laugh or even smile, let alone attempt to have fun with us children. Perhaps, I think now, she was a depressive, and as a result made no attempt to escape the inevitable.

After asking about the fate of our nursemaid, my mother seemed to lose interest in hearing about what Edith had been through. Within a couple of days Edith was just the housemaid, being inducted into her new job. It must have been odd for her to find herself in a strange country and an unfamiliar house, but surrounded by furniture she had known well, long ago and far away, polishing silver and washing dishes she had handled on a daily basis a lifetime ago. Europe lay in ruins, but my mother's KPM china was intact.

I, on the other hand, was agog with questions. What was Berlin like during the war, and how had she managed to stay alive? And why hadn't she liked Palestine, when the rest of the world seemed to be excited by the newly created Israel? But it was difficult during the early days after her arrival. My mother was always hovering around, making sure that her new maid knew where everything was, understood what was expected of her and saw to it that she carried out her duties properly. I found it was better to keep out of the way for the time being.

My brother had almost nothing to do with Edith, for the

simple reason that he had forgotten almost all his German. So he would give her a broad smile, still with a dimple in it, and retreat to his attic. When she referred to Ernst, I explained that he was always called Ernest now, in the English fashion. Her social interaction with my father did not amount to much more. He did not regard domestic servants as his sphere, and besides, he did not arrive home until it was time for the evening meal, when the serving hatch separated them. While the family ate at the dining table, Edith ate her portion at the kitchen table, ready to pass and receive plates and dishes through the hatch as required. Once the kitchen was tidied she vanished until the following morning. Not so very different from the old days in Berlin, except that there the vast spaces had made such estrangement seem natural. Now, living in enforced intimacy in a small house, it felt very different. It is not easy to make oneself invisible in a bedroom that is adjacent to the master bedroom, and where the slightest noise is audible next door. The awful washstand might, to be fair, be a practical necessity, but for me it symbolized the denial of a truth that could no longer be denied: that all human beings are much the same when you get down to bare skin and bone.

Respectful though she was, going quietly about her duties, I think Edith must have felt it too. In fact I know she did. She was hurt that neither of my parents ever invited her

_____

to sit down with them in the living room, perhaps over a cup of tea, and ask her to tell them something of what she had been through since we left Berlin in 1939. They would have had to be tactful about it, obviously, to have taken their cue from her, and perhaps she would have been too shy to say very much. But at least she would have known that they cared, that their door was always open. It would, it seems to me, have been the natural thing to do, even if Edith had come to our house as a total stranger. I thought we had learnt that much during the war, when doors were always open in times of trouble. Why, even my mother had made cups of tea at one o'clock in the morning, night after night, when the neighbours came from upstairs to take shelter in our ground-floor flat.

But that was then. The war was over now. This was 1948, this – apparently – was peacetime normality.

_____

– 2 –

Edith was shy, I realized that fairly early on. She did not speak unless spoken to, so I did my best to draw her out if and when I got the opportunity. Once, when my mother was out of the house, I invited her into my room to admire my treasures. She did not say much, just made a few appreciative noises on seeing my shelves of books, mainly poetry and popular classics, and the wind-up gramophone, another recent cast-off from my Aunt Ruth, with which I now regaled my schoolfriends. She listened patiently to a crackly pre-war recording, probably Noël Coward, which had come with the gift. It brought on her special smile, something I would learn to watch for, like a rare butterfly.

Normally Edith's face was stolidly impassive, the face of someone in the habit of keeping her thoughts to herself. Perhaps it was the result of her orphanage childhood, or went with the job of being a domestic servant, or was simply part of her nature. But every now and then a small smile hovered round her mouth, all the sweeter for being so rare.

If it sounds sentimental, I cannot help it. Her smile was memorable, if only because it did not come easily. I got in

———

the habit of watching for it when we were alone together, noticing the deep groove of her septum. I felt I was coaxing a child sometimes, since she was under five feet tall, and oddly childlike with it.

That was a delusion, of course. Simpletons do not survive the sort of experiences she had been through.

Not long after Edith arrived, my mother began to spend more time out of the house during weekdays. She went shopping, in the modern sense, picking up non-essentials like clothes and things for the house. Once I came home from school and found a pink cotton frock laid out on my bed. I was furious. It had been bad enough when all the family clothing coupons went on curtains for the house, now she had bought me a dress without consulting me. I was not a kid any more, I was only allowed two frocks for the season, and I hated pink. Either I caught her on a good day, or things *really had changed*, because I was allowed to go to the West End and choose an extra dress by myself.

I suppose she also visited friends on those weekday afternoons. And she acquired a dog, a Yorkshire terrier who became the focus of all the affection she was unable to lavish on members of her own family. Billy Bunter was the first of a series of dogs, all adored and spoilt. I came to the conclusion that dogs were, for her, preferable to human beings because they did not answer back, voice their own opinions, but simply gave slavish, slavering devotion. The dog was taken for walkies, leaving Edith alone in the house more often than not.

I saw my chance when I happened to have a free afternoon, and found Edith polishing the silver on the dining-room table. By now I felt I had established a rapport with her, talking to her about this and that when I found her on her own.

So what was it like? I asked, sitting down on a spare chair. In Berlin, after we left?

A long silence.

The french window was open, as it was a fine afternoon. I do remember that. There was the sound of traffic in the distance, coming from the North Circular Road. And a bird hopping through light in the quiet garden, sunlight spilling into the quiet room.

She was reluctant to talk about it. Apart from anything else, I think so much had happened to her in the intervening years that she did not know where to begin.

It was my last job in service, she said finally. Nobody was looking for a housemaid now. They had either left, or were trying to get out of the country.

She was talking about Jews, I knew, who were legally obliged to employ only Jewish maids, if they lived in and were under the age of 45, to avoid the possibility of sex between master and servant, thus defiling the purity of Aryan womanhood.

But I managed to get by for quite a while, doing unofficial jobs. People didn't like Goebbels, and they didn't like his plans for the Jews either. There was a sort of grapevine going, and there were actually plenty of people willing to employ me, at least for a while, caring for an elderly relative, minding small children, cleaning, that sort of thing. Once I even helped out in a family grocery shop. It had a room at the back where I could sleep. Life was getting difficult for everyone, and I never lied about being Jewish. How could I have done, given my identity papers? You keep your mouth shut and I'll do the same, I was told more than once. Who's to know? Sometimes we would agree on some sort of cover story, just in case. I was a country cousin, up from a rural backwater to enjoy the bright lights of Berlin. That sort of thing.

I tried to imagine Edith coping with the situations she was describing. She was quite incapable of lying her way out of danger, which meant that others, almost always women, were taking the initiative.

If I had to leave at short notice, she went on, they usually gave me a contact address, someone who might need help in the house and would not ask too many questions. For a while it really wasn't all that difficult. Young girls who weren't Jewish now thought domestic work beneath them, given the war, and a lot of married women, especially those with children, were finding it difficult to cope on their own, with their husbands already called up. So, no husbands or sons to object to my presence, though I once had to disappear in a hurry when someone's husband came on leave. I once slept in the room of a boy called Siegfried, who had just joined the army. He died at Stalingrad. I know, because his mother hid me after I went underground. She was very bitter, poor woman.

There was silence for a moment. Edith stared out of the window, polishing forgotten. I felt a turmoil of conflicting emotions, but decided to keep quiet.

Of course, she went on eventually, it couldn't go on for ever. I used to go to the cinema a lot, when I wasn't actually working, just hiding out. It meant a few hours of escape, sitting in the dark, watching newsreels or the latest song-and-dance routine, all fancy costumes and a romantic storyline. Most Berliners didn't want the war, you know – they remembered how awful the last one had been. So some of the newsreels of victorious Germans bombing innocent foreigners did not go down too well, were watched in complete silence.

I used to go to the UFA-Palast. It was a show in itself, with all that fantastic lighting and a proper orchestra. But then the Gestapo took it into their heads, one afternoon, to stop the film and check everybody's papers. That was it, as

———

far as I was concerned. Luckily I had a cover story ready for just this eventuality, so I managed to keep the woman I was staying with out of trouble.

Edith stared down at the silver spread out in front of her. She seemed to have lost track of her story.

And then?

I saw she was visibly distressed. Instead of answering she got up, opened the serving hatch and put through handfuls of cutlery, to be washed and dried before going back into the sideboard. I gave her a hand, then followed her into the kitchen.

And then? I persisted.

She dropped a handful of forks on the kitchen table and sat down suddenly on the low sill of the window overlooking the garden.

And then I had to go and live in a *Judenhaus*. One of those places they put Jews who had been turned out of their own homes. It was awful. I can't begin to tell you. Overcrowded, everybody crammed together, having to share kitchen and bathroom. It wasn't so much the lack of space, though that was bad enough. People's nerves were on edge, arguments would break out over the slightest thing. Frau A would accuse Herr B of stealing her bread ration, that sort of thing. One old lady tried to commit suicide, twice. She succeeded at the third attempt. Nobody knew what was coming next, but everyone feared the worst.

———

———

Rumours were going round. I was working for a shopkeeper, just before the forced labour started, and she made me promise not to go if I was called up to go on a transport. Said she would hide me in the room at the back of the shop. Her soldier son had just come back from the eastern front and told her awful stories about what was going on out there, what they were doing to the Jews. Or was that later? I'm not sure. Said she'd keep food for me if I had to go and work in a factory, and I reckoned that they'd keep us alive as long as we were needed for war work. So I didn't go underground, not then. But I kept in touch.

Edith remembered the silver, and I decided to help with the drying-up. I wanted to hear what it had been like, doing slave labour in a munitions factory.

It was hard, she told me. Ten hours at a stretch. I think they were trying to work us to death. The word got round that some factories were better than others. AEG and Siemens treated their Jewish workers well, I. G. Farben did not. As luck would have it my first job was at I. G. Farben, making silk for parachutes. It meant hours of standing, watching the spindles to make sure the threads did not break, and the machine room was hot and noisy. In the end I managed to get myself dismissed because I started going sick with abdominal pains – all that standing. The next job was better, and the foreman was really nice. Saved our lives, in the end.

———

———

Really?

I stopped drying up for a moment. Edith gave that subtle little smile of hers.

His name was Hans Klennermann. Remember that name. We were working with electrical components, a fiddly job, but you could do it sitting down at the conveyor belt. They went into aeroplanes eventually, the bits we were working on. Luftwaffe bombers. Hans was a bit of a flirt, and he made terrible jokes about the Nazis, could have got him into serious trouble. But he was popular, and he wasn't the only one to take a crack at the Nazis when he knew himself to be among friends.

And then, as the two of us put the silver back in the sideboard, she told me about the notorious *Fabrikaktion*. Early in 1943 Goebbels decided he could dispense with Jewish labour, since there were by now enough slave workers from foreign countries. Berlin was full of them, doing all sorts of jobs. Anyhow, one day, when it was time to knock off, Hans Klennermann told Edith and the other Jewish workers not to report for work on the following morning. Which was the day that lorries arrived all over the city to pick up Jewish workers for deportation. Klennermann was not the only person to warn his Jewish workers.

It was at this point, Edith explained, that she obviously did have to go underground.

I heard a key turn in the lock of the front door.

———

———

Frau Unger, said Edith.

Time to disappear, I said, giggling. And wandered off into the garden while Edith went back to the kitchen, greeting my mother *en route*.

I overheard snatches of conversation. My mother sounded pleased with herself, having had a successful shopping trip. Greeted the dog, who yapped excitedly. I wandered nonchalantly into the hall, peered into shopping bags, made approving noises, saw Edith standing at the kitchen door waiting to be told what to do. Instructions duly followed. Some tea, no doubt, followed by vegetables for the evening meal.

She was in a good mood that afternoon, I remember. Did I miss an opportunity? Could I have brokered some kind of understanding between the two of them? But Edith, being Edith, had already vanished into the kitchen, to do as she was told. And my mother, being who she was, had nothing further to say.

———

– 3 –

I come from a family of secular Jews and, apart from a temporary love affair with Christianity, the result of an English education, have no faith of any kind. Yet until recently I made a point of calling myself Jewish, partly because I felt that Hitler had made me one, but also to avoid being labelled German. Anything but that. The history of the Third Reich meant that I was absolved from wearing the badge of shame the rest of them would have to endure. Time and some of my more recent writing, including this book, have helped to change all that. I have made my peace with the country in which I was born and acknowledge the fact that I was born there, without caveat.

The problem of collective responsibility had troubled me while I was still growing up, ever since my father came back after the war, swearing never to set foot in Germany again. It was his diehard attitude to his own generation of Germans that bothered me. But, I once asked him, what would you have done if you had not been Jewish? It was obvious to me that being a Jew absolved anyone who was otherwise a German national of all responsibility except as a victim. Not my problem, he answered shortly, putting an end to the conversation, but I thought otherwise. I had almost said 'if you had not been lucky enough to be a Jew', but I knew that was going too far.

Head and heart, however, do not always concur. I might understand intellectually that not all Germans were murdering criminals, but for many years I felt an unspoken bitterness which I kept to myself. Where did complicity begin and end? I remember, as a young woman, going out of my way to be polite and friendly to a German woman, but only to highlight the difference between us. When I was told that she had been very impressed by my behaviour, I pretended not to know why. Stories of German suffering during the war left me unmoved: Serves you right was my unspoken thought, never having seen a German child dug out of bomb rubble. At the age of eight I did see the twisted remains of a German fighter plane shot down in Cirencester Park, during my year of evacuation. It made me think, for the first time, that the pilot might have ended up just as mangled. But that was 1940, and by 1945, knowing about the death camps, I was less tender-hearted.

Germany has of course changed over the past half-century, perhaps more so than other countries, precisely because of its history. In the old days I would lie about my origins to strangers on my first visits to Berlin, and anyone of

———

a certain age was a possible war criminal as far as I was concerned. Now I am quite open about my past, and have to reassure a younger generation that, really, they have nothing to feel bad about. Time, and the birth of children and their children, helps to bring about change, but even that is not always enough to heal old wounds. The silence, the lies and prevarications established half a century ago have to be overcome, and that can be very hard. I always knew that I ought to find out where and how my grandparents had died, and I always had excuses. Finally, out of the blue, by now myself a grandmother, I found myself weeping, unable to stop.

I did what I had to do, asked for and got the necessary information, but the tears, kept back for so long, refused to stop. I decided I had no alternative other than to write a book, being a writer. I made half a dozen attempts, threw them all away. The world and his wife had been here before, bookshelves were laden with what were often very amateurish, predictable memoirs. It was only when I decided to write as a grandmother, remembering her own grandmother, that I found a way in, and the result was curiously comforting. I felt that not only I, but my grandparents, whom I had mourned for so long, were at last at peace.

At long last head and heart had synchronized, could function in harmony, not at odds with each other.

I think it is for this reason that it is only now, after half a

———

century, that I can recognize the significance of what Edith had to tell me all those years ago. So many odd stories, so many strange reunions belong to that period just after the war, and my prime interest in Edith at the time was her connection with my early childhood in Berlin, my second the fact that she had been to the newly created Israel and been bitterly disappointed. I chose not to think at length about the fact that she had survived as an illegal in wartime Berlin, even though she had no money.

I already knew one person who had been 'hidden' by Germans for most of the war: my wealthy paternal grand-mother. But Unger Omi's situation could not have been more different from that of a penniless housemaid. To me my grandmother's story only proved what was already well known, that the Nazis liked nothing better than to rob rich Jews of everything they had. In the case of my grand-mother, it was a Swiss bank account that saved her. As early as 1943 we were contacted by an elderly lady, Frau Landsberg, who had hit the British headlines after being allowed out of Germany on an exchange basis, by virtue of the fact that her deceased husband had left England at the age of two but retained his British citizenship, which his widow and their unmarried daughter, Gerda, still enjoyed. So both arrived in Britain halfway through the war, and what they had to say about life in Germany, with the war now going against them, was obviously of great interest to journalists and the BBC. I had read about her myself.

Frau Landsberg contacted our family and told us that my grandmother was still alive, and that there was a plan afoot to get her and a dozen other wealthy Jews out of Germany – this at a time when Berlin had been officially declared *Judenrein* by Goebbels.

Through the good offices of a Swiss bank, an arrangement had been made for these officially non-existent Jews to buy a shoe factory in Guatemala from a patriotic Nazi eager to return to the fatherland in its hour of need, in return for safe conduct to a neutral country. Switzerland, we now know, was not too keen on Jews, often turned refugees away at the border, and was responsible for getting the conspicuous J put on German passports to make their job easier. The Swiss also allowed trainloads of arrested Jews to pass through their territory under cover of darkness. On the other hand they were keen to do business with high-ranking Nazis at a time when normal business was at a low ebb.

Frau Landsberg, a 'cultivated' elderly lady whose only fault seemed to be an open contempt for her daughter (who was admittedly dull and unattractive), became a friend of the family and, for me, a surrogate grandmother. I liked to sit at her feet, shod in black patent-leather shoes, so similar to those both my missing grandmothers had worn, and listen to her educated talk. But my father treated her story with scepticism.

Fast-forward to the summer of 1944. The Allies had just landed in Normandy, and my father was home on embarcation leave prior to driving his lorry on to the newly conquered beaches, when the doorbell rang. I went to the door, took the telegram and handed it to my father, who was shaving, naked to the waist, in the bathroom. He sat down suddenly on the edge of the bath, and my mother put an arm round his bare shoulder in a rare moment of intimacy. My grandmother was in Stockholm. She was to die in her sleep a few months later, but at least she died in bed. Sadly, she did not live long enough – only a matter of weeks – to know that her daughter Margot and the two boys, hiding in the French countryside, were alive and well. Paris was liberated in August, but it was not until my father managed to reach his sister's flat that he was told the good news by the concierge. My grandmother died in September, and her last letter to my father was full of anxiety about their fate. She was also contrite at having added to my father's worries by her refusal to leave Germany while there was still time. That she should have decided to stay in Germany, presumably sure that nothing would ever disturb her lifestyle – even after the last of her children, my Aunt Lotte, decided to go – confirms what all her offspring said of her: that she was extremely self-centred, and always had been.

Having read Anne Frank's diary, I had visualized my grandmother cooped up for months on end in a dark, stuffy attic. I should have realized that this was very far from the truth when her luggage arrived in London after the war – not the overnight bag we had been expecting but fourteen suitcases crammed with brand-new items, many of them presents obviously intended for the family. There was fancy table linen and jewellery, including three pearl necklaces for the women in the family and a coral necklace for little Eva, by now far too old for anything so babyish.

Where did she find such things at a time when Berlin was suffering acute shortages of every kind? She had obviously done some serious shopping before leaving the country, like the Queen of Sheba. To say that she was hidden at all seems like an overstatement. She was useful to the Nazis, and they knew where to find her.

In an atmosphere of disbelief the family gathered one afternoon to share out the contents of the suitcases. One thing, I remember, really did puzzle my father. My grandmother had been a diabetic, who needed daily insulin injections. Who on earth had supplied them, and kept her alive all those years?

Edith would eventually give me the answer.

So then what happened?

I had got home from school and found Edith alone in the house, shelling peas for the evening meal.

After the *Fabrikaktion*. When you went underground.

Edith looked vague, slightly bewildered, as though she had forgotten our recent conversation. I put the kettle on for tea, set out cups and saucers for us both.

Does it bother you to talk about all this?

Something about her manner suddenly made me uneasy. Perhaps I was stirring memories she would rather try to forget.

It's OK, she said slowly. Well, the first thing I did was to take off my yellow star. Obviously. Though I was careful to keep it. I sewed it into the hem of my overcoat. For later, when the Allies came.

She took a first sip of tea, bit into a biscuit.

I couldn't walk round the streets wearing that any more, if I was going to become a U-boat.

I stared at her in disbelief.

———

Walk round the streets?

I was so ashamed when we first had to start wearing them. I didn't know where to look. But it was all quite different from what I'd imagined. I mean people were embarrassed for us, if you know what I mean. It was as if *they* were ashamed. Because we were doing war work we were permitted to travel by tram, but we weren't allowed to sit down. Jews always had to stand. Well, the first morning I had the yellow star on my coat – and I didn't dare to cover it up, like some people did – a man got up and offered me his seat. I tried to refuse, but he wouldn't take no for an answer. It happened quite often after that; women too. Sometimes, of course, there was standing room only. Once a woman pushed herself up close to me and put an apple in my pocket. Another time it was cigarettes. Once I even got a note with an address on it, though I never dared to use it. I kept it though, just in case I had nowhere else to go. Luckily something, somewhere, always seemed to turn up.

What sort of thing?

People to take you in.

Like Hans Klennermann? I suggested. I was teasing, remembering what she had told me before.

But Edith shook her head, her smile rueful.

He was killed in an air raid, when the bombing started. The whole factory was gutted.

I've lost count really, Edith went on in the ensuing silence. So many people. Sometimes it was just for a couple of nights, sometimes for several weeks. I've slept in an outhouse, in a laundry room, several kitchens, and a printing works for blind people where nobody was doing any work. The important thing was to keep on the move, so neighbours wouldn't get suspicious. I'd be told not to turn the lights on, or only flush the toilet at certain times. There seemed to be a network of people who would suddenly turn up out of nowhere and take you to a new hiding place. Once I even slept in a boathouse on the Havel in the middle of winter. It was freezing, I can tell you. But only for a few nights.

The important thing was to look as though you were going somewhere. Purposeful stride, that sort of thing. I'd go to the Ku'damm and look at the window displays, even though there was nothing to buy and in any case I didn't have any money. Sometimes I went to the Tiergarten and fed the ducks, if I was lucky enough to have a bit of stale bread to spare. After a bit I even started going to the cinema again, though I was scared at first, and kept an eye on the door. But it was warm in there, it passed the time and took my mind off things. Except for the newsreels, of course. German tanks rolling into foreign countries, killing people who had never done the Germans any harm. The triumphant propaganda. I would wait for Zara Leander to

———

start singing so I could feel happy again, forget everything for an hour or two.

So you still went out, in spite of everything?

Of course, said Edith, getting up to throw the peapods into the bin, then adding hot water to the teapot. It was the only way to keep sane. The mother of a friend of mine used to go for walks, wearing a widow's veil to avoid suspicion. Women in black were a common sight by this time, so nobody knew what she looked like, and of course they respected her grief. Her noble sacrifice for the Fatherland. Besides, it was important to keep in touch with other people who had gone underground. There were one or two cafés where the illegals could exchange useful information, though you had to be careful, keep an eye on the door. The Gestapo knew about these places, of course, and might choose that particular afternoon to pay a visit, bringing 'the blonde Lorelei', or some other Jewish traitor who had made a deal with the Gestapo, betraying people to save their own skins. They say she wore a green hat, the Lorelei, though I never saw her.

What sort of information? I asked. Seeing Edith now, it was difficult to imagine her in this other world, getting by.

The best place to get forged papers, for a start. If you had those it made everything a lot easier.

And what sort of people did you go to?

I had forgotten all about the time, and so, I think, had

———

Edith. At any moment now we might be interrupted by someone coming through the front door.

Well, the police were often very helpful.

The *police?*

This whole story was getting increasingly bizarre. If I did not know Edith was too innocent, too naïve to spin a yarn, I would have suspected her of making the whole thing up.

Edith laughed, actually grinned when she saw the expression on my face.

Not the Gestapo, you *Dummkopf*. The ordinary, local police. They were usually very helpful, if you told them you had lost your papers in an air raid or something. They'd give you a blank form and let you get on with it, give yourself a new identity. All you needed was a rubber stamp, and if they didn't give it to you a forger could do it, transfer the old stamp with a hard-boiled egg, that sort of thing. It all got a lot easier as the air raids got worse, so many people really had lost their homes, ration cards, everything. And the police could not check up on you, even if they wanted to, since they no longer had access to central records. Things were falling apart, the whole organization, and everybody knew it. So I became Hedwig Schmidt from Pomerania. Couldn't find anyone to dye my hair, but it didn't seem to matter. That's when I went to work for the shopkeeper I told you about. I'd help serve customers and sleep in the back at

night. It was nice. Everyone was very friendly, asked no awkward questions, and there was lots of food going spare, until
the whole area was flattened by Allied bombers and there
were no customers left, so Frau Körner shut up shop. She
was very sorry, but she did manage to find another place for
me to stay, if only for a few days.

I suddenly remembered my grandmother and her dia-
betes, and my father's puzzlement as to how she had been
kept alive during that period.

You remember my grandmother, my father's mother?

Frau Doktor Unger? Of course.

Edith had stacked our teacups in the sink and was fetching potatoes from the larder.

Well, she was hidden in Berlin until 1944, and she was
diabetic. Who looked after her – got her the insulin she
needed?

Oranienburger Strasse, Edith answered promptly, starting in on the potatoes. Word soon got around that the
doctors' surgery there helped illegals. Secretly of course,
mostly after dark. When medicines were needed they would
use free samples they got from drug companies, or one of
their legal patients would volunteer to go to the chemist
with a prescription, pretending to be sick. That must have
been what they did for Frau Doktor Unger, since she had to
have insulin every day. You couldn't go there, of course, or
only in an emergency, to get a message through. By that

———

time most of the telephones weren't working and anyhow, you never knew who was listening in. Someone would come after dark and give a special knock. I had very bad bronchitis one winter. Most people got sick in the winter, what with no heating, hardly any food, and most of the houses damaged by the raids, one way or another. Windows boarded, leaking roofs, you name it. The summers weren't so bad. I could go scavenging for fresh vegetables on the allotments, but not in winter, with the ground frozen solid, and nothing edible to be found. People started going to the Tiergarten for firewood, or breaking up what was left of their furniture, to try and keep warm. Coal supplies could not get through in really bad weather, stuck in the ice. I wouldn't be here today if it had not been for the staff at the clinic, who came night after night, even after the air-raid warning had sounded.

By that time I was spending most of my time in the cellar. About six of us were more or less living down there, so it was rather overcrowded. The top of the house had been completely blown away in an air raid but we used to come up in the daytime to cook in the kitchen, if and when the power came on. Often there was no water either, and we'd have to fetch it in buckets. Washing was a luxury.

One bath a week my mother now allowed her.

We took turns in the kitchen to get washed. Washed our

———

clothes too, and hung them up to dry. We must have been pretty smelly, but the whole city stank. Gas leaks, bodies under the rubble.

I stared at her wet stubby fingers, dipping a freshly peeled potato into clean water for a final rinse.

Who's 'we'? I asked, getting up to let in the dog, who was scratching at the kitchen door. Were you all illegal Jews?

Good heavens no.

Edith gave the dog one of our biscuits and watched him make short work of it, licking up the last crumbs from the linoleum.

I was the only one.

And they knew?

Of course. There was a young boy who was terrified of being called up and sent to the eastern front. By this time there were a lot of deserters, even though it was punishable by death. And boys who saw no point in being called up, when the war was so clearly lost. A woman with a daughter, father killed or missing. They'd already been bombed out twice. There was one woman, a Party member, who objected strongly to my presence at first, but seemed to change her mind after a bit. Perhaps she saw I wasn't really that bad, but there may have been other reasons.

A pause. Edith gave her little smile. Dried her hands and put the pan full of potatoes on the stove.

Everyone knew the war was lost, that the Allies were coming, and that terrible crimes had been committed, especially against the Jews, which would have to be accounted for. Given the situation, helping to save the life of a Jew could do you no end of good, later, when the day of reckoning came.

With the war coming to an end, even a poor Jew had his or her uses, said Edith, her head half hidden in the larder. Don't get me wrong, she added, coming up for air with an onion, most of the time I was glad to help. People had been very good to me, often at some risk to themselves, but I can think of one or two people who just wanted their *Persilschein*.

I looked puzzled. My German was letting me down.

Waschpulver. Washing powder. 'Persil washes whiter,' she added in hesitant English, obviously having studied the ubiquitous billboards. I think it was the first complete English sentence I had so far heard her utter. I burst out laughing.

Edith joined in, at least her smile broadened. Berliners make good jokes, she told me, even when times are bad. Especially then. As for the *Persilschein*, that was after the Allies took over. Jews who had managed to survive got special privileges, extra rations, a decent room if you were in luck. Everybody else had to be given a clean bill of health, prove they had not collaborated with the Nazis. I would be asked to say they had been good to me, helped me out at some point, given me food, hidden me, and many of them had. As for the rest— She shrugged. Often I just felt sorry for them.

You *what*? Righteous indignation came easily to me in those days.

You have no idea, Evchen, just how terrible everything was. I'm glad your grandmother managed to get out when she did. Nothing but death and destruction. You couldn't recognize your own street any more, let alone expect to find your own front door. No public transport, no water or electricity most of the time, streets impassable because of the rubble. The top brass, of course, had all left by then. You could go and watch them packing their belongings into lorries on the Wilhelmstrasse. The foreign workers, with nothing left to do, with factories all out of action, would go and jeer at them. And it was these foreigners, the slave workers, as often as not, who helped to put out fires and dug people out of the rubble after a raid, dead or alive. People who had taken shelter in the underground drowned when water mains burst. I myself saw dead children being brought out . . .

Edith lapsed into a silence I did not know how to break.

It had suddenly got very dark, rainclouds gathering beyond the kitchen window. I got up to switch on the light, checked the time on my wristwatch. It was a man's watch which my father had brought back from occupied Germany. My first watch, still a luxury item in England, but obtainable over there for a few cigarettes, army issue.

And then the Russians, she went on. Everyone was afraid of them. So the trains going west, those still running, were always crammed.

Her eyes were red, watering from the onion she had been peeling. She wiped down the kitchen table, threw the outer skin, brown and brittle, into the kitchen bin.

I was warned not to try. The Gestapo, they said, were still checking trains for illegal Jews, even now.

It had begun to rain, blurring everything beyond the window.

So I thought, she went on, her back to me, how bad could it be . . .

Edith lapsed into silence. All we could hear was the rain, getting heavier by the minute.

I had heard about the Russians, what they did to women. And decided it was time to go upstairs and make a start on my homework. It was best not to ask certain questions.

I slept badly that night, I remember. I recalled the news-reel photographs of Berlin after the final defeat, the aerial shots of roofless buildings, mile after mile. I remembered my grandmother's last passport photo, the gaunt old woman who looked twice her real age, how my father had picked it out of the luggage on that post-war afternoon when the family went through her things. My father had ripped it up at once, but not before I had seen it, sitting on the arm of his chair, looking over his shoulder. That image belied the luxury items spread out before us. The plump woman of her last pre-war portrait, neat white hair carefully backlit, had shrunk to this unrecognizable, half-starved crone.

I lay in bed and thought of the faces, the places on the other side of the divide, the dark river of death – Styx, English Channel, call it what you will – and tried to count them: the woman who sold us cauliflowers on the Wittenbergplatz, the *Schupo* who stopped the traffic on the corner so we could cross safely. Fräulein Minna who kept house for my grandparents and always had a smile when I came to see the Dutch tiles in the kitchen, the conductor on the tram to school who made sure I got off at the right stop: Roseneck. The shops we had been to, and the women who worked in them and sold us things, all of them smiling, helpful and polite. In particular the person who helped my grandparents choose a gold bracelet for me, with a medallion depicting one of the cherubs on the Sistine Madonna, who had to lean over the counter to catch sight of me, I was so small.

And Edith, just one of the many, the countless faces

without names who had been part of a vanished world from which I had escaped. From which Edith too, who had a name, had also surfaced once more, clinging to us after the shipwreck.

THREE

– 1 –

I remember the summer of 1948 as a pleasurable one. I had passed my General School Certificate a year earlier, when I was only fifteen, so with three years in the sixth form I could take things easy for the time being. Materially, life was improving too. My father had bought a Morris Minor and there were regular trips into the countryside at weekends, at a time when roads were still blessedly empty, and motoring was fun. We picked bluebells, had picnics, and paid regular visits to a farm which sold us fresh eggs to supplement our meagre ration. I went on outings with schoolfriends and saved up my pocket money to sit in the gods at the Haymarket, now that London theatres were coming back to life.

Edith had a free half-day during the week, but did not use it. I did persuade her, when she first arrived, to look at the Houses of Parliament and Big Ben, but after that she seemed to lose interest in sightseeing.

Whenever I got home from school she would be sitting, by herself, in an empty house. Sitting in the kitchen, often with nothing to do. It did not take me long to realize that she was waiting for me.

_____

Because my mother had failed her, Edith had developed a dependency on me. I knew that Edith should be getting out of the house in her free time, going to English classes, making friends with people in a similar situation, but my mother had done nothing about it, and Edith seemed to lack the willpower to do anything on her own behalf. I thought about talking to my mother about it, but knew it was worse than hopeless. She would take umbrage, get annoyed with me for not minding my own business or, worse still, take her annoyance out on Edith, who was too vulnerable to speak up for herself.

So I did nothing. Or rather, I went on going to the kitchen as soon as I got back from school, to listen to her woes. By now these were quite explicit. She was all alone in the world, and I was her only friend. Frau Unger ignored her, did not talk to her except to give instructions. If only, she said on one occasion, I would hurry up and get married, then she could come and work for me. I did not answer, but it became clear to me that Edith did not live in the real world. She was stuck in the past. At sixteen I had no intention of getting married in the near future, and, when I did, there would certainly be no live-in housemaid. The woman she had worked for before the war no longer existed, and she had come in search of a memory, possibly idealized with time.

It was at this point in our relationship, burdened with

her misery, that I asked about her family and found out for the first time that she had been brought up in an orphanage. No hope there then: she really was all alone in the world. But, to be fair to her, Edith had not begun her quest for a new beginning by getting in touch with my mother. She had first gone as an illegal immigrant to Palestine, and written to us from there. And if there was one bit of news that dominated the headlines that spring and summer, it was the creation of Israel. I knew very little about it, and cared less, but the bits I saw on cinema newsreels looked very upbeat, full of sunshine and hope. Lots of Jews seemed genuinely thrilled.

I knew almost nothing about the Middle East, but I did know that getting to Palestine in 1947 must have required considerable initiative and courage. So what went wrong? Why did she leave after going to all that trouble? Her immediate answer shocked me.

Because, she said, staring out at the cloudy northern sky on the other side of the kitchen window, now showing a few drops of rain, everybody hates everybody else.

I do not know what I expected, but not this. Something about the climate maybe, or that she was homesick for Europe. It was unlike Edith to be so bitterly judgemental. And it ran contrary to everything that the new Israel was supposed to stand for, to the smiling faces I had seen on the newsreels. But years later, when I began the research for this book, I found that Edith's words had been echoed by other people who had visited the area either during the war, before Israel came into being, or during the difficult years just before or after 1948. British people who happened to find themselves stuck there during the war years, like the novelist Olivia Manning, or officials with the unenviable job of trying to make the Mandate work, or hapless Jewish refugees fleeing from Hitler but without a prior interest in Zionism – all to a greater or lesser degree were disturbed by what they found. Not just a bitter hostility between Jews and Arabs, but Jews who seemed to have nothing in common except their religion, and not always that. By the time I started to do my background reading for this book I was no longer the naïve schoolgirl of 1948, and I realized that Palestine could never have offered Edith what she was looking for at the end of the war, when she found herself quite alone in the world.

By the time, during the last decade, that I started to interest myself in Edith's story, it was precisely her negative reaction to Israel that interested me. I do not think there has ever been a time when I did not think that the creation of Israel was a historical mistake, unfair on the Arabs, who were in no way responsible for the Holocaust. I have never really believed that 'making two blades of grass grow where one grew before' justified the occupation of somebody else's territory. Events in recent years have long since dissipated

———

the utopian, socialist vision of the early years that sent so many young people off to work on a kibbutz, and other British Jews to settle there. So many decades have passed since 1948, and a whole mendacious mythology has arisen around the creation of Israel. Increasingly angry at the situation in the Middle East and the plight of the Palestinians, I thought Edith's story would help to expose the truth. She was duped, but so were thousands of others.

———

– 2 –

Over the years a myth has arisen that Israel was created because a guilty world wanted to atone for the mass murder of the Jews. On the contrary, Israel came into being largely as a result of pressure from the United States, to take care of a continuing problem: those Jews who had been rounded up for murder but were still alive when the war came to an end. They were known as 'displaced persons', DPs for short, and to be honest, the world did not want them.

However, this is primarily Edith's story, and she was not a displaced person. To begin with, she was once again a German citizen on German soil. She had not even been in a concentration camp, an *a priori* condition if the Allies were to treat you as a DP. The yellow star which she had so carefully preserved in the hem of her shabby overcoat would, on the other hand, have ensured that she got special treatment from the authorities, whichever sector of Berlin she found herself in.

Her problems were primarily emotional, both then and later, when she came to us.

Edith's situation in 1945 was odd. On the one hand she

owed her life to the kindness of Germans, many of them initially strangers who took risks on her behalf. On the other, it was hardly possible to forget that it was Germans, her fellow countrymen, who had organized and carried out the Holocaust. My mother had a cousin who, with her daughter, survived the death camps, though her elderly mother did not. A few years after the war my mother visited her in Berlin, and described her as 'living in a gilded cage, hating everybody'. Her daughter eventually married a German, so presumably came to terms with the past. Edith, on the other hand, had nobody, no relative of any sort. And both age and temperament made it unlikely that she would find herself a marriage partner.

Once the war was over her loneliness must have been acute. During the war the problem of survival had been an end in itself. You took one day at a time, coping with its difficulties, and thought no further ahead. There was no point anyhow: anything could happen, and probably would. And there had always been people ready and willing to help her, now that the war was almost over. Not just because she might, when the time came, put in a good word on their behalf, but because the misery of trying to survive during those final months was increasingly felt by everybody.

But once the war was truly over and Berlin sectioned off by the Allies, a new kind of normality was gradually established. Life was difficult for the surviving population, largely made up of women, children and old men. Food was desperately short and the city lay in ruins. Gangs of women cleared the endless rubble, brick by brick, using only their bare hands. Mothers foraged for food and fuel to feed their children, found the occasional trophy among the rubble, an item of clothing, perhaps, or a usable saucepan. Wives worried about husbands who had failed to return from the eastern front. The trams did not run, the taps were often dry, horses dropped dead in the street and were rapidly carved up for food.

The people who had for so long helped Edith to survive gradually drifted off, preoccupied by their own not inconsiderable problems. Edith no longer needed them: she was one of the lucky ones now, and quite right too. The old companionship, based on hardship and fear and a growing hatred of the regime, gradually faded. Where were they now, the people with whom she had sat night after night, listening to the drone of Lancaster bombers, the sickening whistle prior to the explosion which meant that someone else, not you, had copped it? Where was the prostitute who had offered her services free to Russian soldiers, to spare someone's innocent young daughter? Or the Nazi woman with a Party card who had begun by objecting to sharing the cellar with a Jew, but later reported her dead so that nobody would come looking for her? Either they had left town or they were back in what was left of their old homes, patching holes in the roof, bartering their missing men's watches for a few cigarettes, the new currency.

Meanwhile I wore the watch of some young man who had not come home. He, whoever he was, had no use for it, and it got me to school on time. Was it in 1948 that I got my first lady's watch for my birthday? I was a young lady now, conscious of my appearance, and the fashion that year was for curved glass and narrow leather straps. The dead soldier's watch went in the dustbin. Junk, like last year's sandals.

Edith went to see one or two people who had been kind to her in the past, but it was awkward. They seemed pleased to see her, and accepted any little gifts she might bring – biscuits, or sweets for the children – readily enough. But the old camaraderie was no longer there. She even sensed a hint of embarrassment, perhaps because of who she was. The Allies had made sure that every German citizen knew, beyond a shadow of a doubt, what had been done to the Jews in their name.

Edith felt lonely as never before, abandoned. She now had a neat little flat, overlooking an empty field near the airport, but she found the solitude oppressive. There were no shops or cinemas nearby, and because of her status she was excused from standing in line with the other women in their

———

headscarves, tossing dusty bricks from hand to hand. The job did not appeal to her anyway, and she already felt, without being able to put it into words, that rebuilding the city in which she had been born would not be part of her future. Often she sat for hours in her little apartment, staring out at the field on the other side of the road, listening to the sound of planes landing or taking off at nearby Tempelhof. She cried quite a bit, without really knowing why.

She thought, vaguely, about taking a job, only what? She often took trips into the centre, where there was life and movement of a sort, where she felt at home, despite the destruction. One or two cafés had reopened, largely for the benefit of occupying soldiers, but she knew she had neither the looks nor the confidence to wait at tables. Besides, one look at the women who were working in these places told her it was not just coffee, ersatz or genuine, they were willing to sell.

She went, twice a week, to look at the lists, of survivors and of the dead. That was how she knew, quite early on, that Schwester Eva, our nursemaid, was dead of typhus, and with the knowledge another hope was gone. She would look at the faces of others studying the lists, but recognize nobody, only the reflection of her own blank misery. She was told to come back, the lists were being updated all the time, but by now she was numb. Who was she looking for anyway? Even if she did find someone, would it matter,

———

———

either to them or to her? Even Eva had not been a close friend, it was just circumstances that had brought them together at a particular time, nothing more special. The truth was, she had nobody to lose.

Nevertheless she kept coming back. Because there was nothing else to do. Because she did not belong anywhere else, except among those anxious faces, other illegals who had now resurfaced, looking for information. Now and then she saw Allied soldiers, either GIs or men from the British Army, looking for relatives they had left behind when they themselves escaped from Nazi Germany.

———

– 3 –

I never knew, said Edith, that there were so many Jews in the world. There are Jews as far away as Russia, did you know that? I had no idea, not till the Ivans arrived. All the Germans were terrified of them, and those who could not get out of Berlin tried to hide. Especially the women. No woman was safe from them. But sometimes, if they were in a good mood, they would give you food. Once, when an Ivan found his way into our cellar, the others told him I was a Jew, and that he should leave me alone. But do you know what he did? He kissed me on both cheeks, showed me a photograph of his mother and kept saying *Yid, evrei,* pointing to himself, to explain that he too was a Jew. And then he started to cry.

Edith shook her head in disbelief.

I think he was a bit drunk, she added. I could smell vodka.

I was less afraid of them after that. I knew I would probably be all right if I showed them my yellow star. Unless they were very drunk, in which case it was fairly easy to give them the slip.

———

As for the GIs, lots of them were Jewish, with German names. I would see them looking through the lists of Jewish survivors. I still went every few days, more for something to do than in the hopes of finding anyone I knew. And in the end I did meet someone. Elsa Cohen. We had been at the orphanage together, and kept in touch later too, for a while, going on group outings, that sort of thing. And there she was, large as life, staring at me. 'Edith?' Well, you can imagine, both of us lost for words, then both talking at once. Elsa had trained as a pioneer for Palestine quite early on, learning about agriculture. I knew that, but I didn't know she had actually managed to get out there before the war. Now she was back, to recruit survivors for a new life in what would soon become Israel, the Jewish nation state.

Our moment has come, Elsa had said, gripping my arm. She certainly looked well on it, sunburnt and fit, like an athlete.

From what Edith told me, it was obvious that Elsa had been very persuasive. That was her job and, to be fair, she really believed in the Zionist cause. In the post-war period quite a few Jews who had settled in Palestine before the war were sent back to Europe to recruit survivors, but most of them were hard at work in the camps, especially those run by Americans, trying to sign up the tired, dispirited and increasingly demoralized ex-prisoners with nowhere to go.

And even here there was a problem, since the US and Britain were at loggerheads over the issue. Britain, it seems, was the enemy now, with gunboats patrolling the Mediterranean to stop dispossessed Jews reaching their new and rightful homeland. That was Elsa's version of events. But, she went on, the recruiters had all sorts of ruses for bypassing their army and navy. Meanwhile the American authorities actively encouraged the visiting Zionists, who often took over the running of the DP camps, until recently German concentration camps, signed up inmates for political parties they knew nothing about, introduced kosher food in the kitchens and made sure any children embarked on a Jewish education. The discipline they introduced did help to improve morale, which was at a low ebb. Most of the DPs had come from eastern Europe, where they were not wanted, and where they had no desire to return. And so they lingered in the hated camps, while the rest of the world argued about what to do with them.

Elsa had bumped into Edith by pure chance. She had come to Berlin by way of a detour, on a personal visit, to see what, if anything, was left of her home city and who, if anyone, was left of the Jewish community, of which she had once been an active member. Far from depressing her, what she saw and heard only buoyed up her self-confidence, told her how right she had been to go to Palestine a decade earlier. Life out there had its difficulties, but nothing that could not be overcome, especially now that the Jews who had earlier refused the call to Eretz Israel had been so severely punished for their lack of faith.

If Elsa was jubilant, Edith had never been so depressed. She had survived the war, the deportations, the relentless bombing of Berlin, but for what? Looking at the lists of the dead who would never return from Auschwitz, Sachsenhausen or wherever only emphasized what she already knew in her bones: she was quite alone in the world. Nobody loved her, nobody wanted her, no one was looking through those lists in the hope of finding her named as a survivor. Even Elsa, who seemed pleased to see her, had only bumped into her by chance.

And so, perhaps inevitably, Edith was putty in her hands. She saw a vision, the possibility of a new beginning in a new land, where she truly would belong. A Jew among Jews, one big family, sharing all things in common. She was told about the kibbutz movement, where she would be part of a community, and would never need to feel alone again. She remembered the Russian soldier who had kissed her on both cheeks and shown her a picture of his mother; the British soldier called Rosenberg who picked her up in his arms and whirled her in the air with delight just because she was alive;

the GI from Dahlem who wept when he found his grand-mother's name on the lists of the dead and spoke to her in halting, childish German.

For the first time in months Edith got excited, her pulse quickened. She invited Elsa to her little flat in Tempelhof and watched as the other woman, with her tanned skin and sun-bleached hair, looked round the dingy walls, which had not seen a lick of paint in years, and stared out of the living-room window at the field opposite, green and empty under a cloudy sky.

Very nice, she said finally, dropping into the only chair, but just what are you going to do here?

And Edith had to admit she had no idea. She was thinking of getting a second chair, but who would sit in it? She had a bed, a chair and a table. What else had she ever had?

Elsa pressed home her advantage.

Think you'll find a job as a housemaid, waiting on some damned Germans, cleaning up their shit?

Elsa took Edith to meet a colleague of hers, who gave lectures in what was left of the Jewish community centre in Fasanenstrasse, a ruin among all the other ruins. Only a few came to listen, since most had plans to join relatives in various parts of the world, from the US to South America. Edith, having no relatives, decided to make world Jewry her family, and go to Palestine with Elsa.

– 4 –

From what Edith told me in our Hendon kitchen, Elsa was clearly a rather formidable woman. There was regret in her voice as she told me about her.

I trusted her, she said sadly, fidgeting nervously with a tea towel as she spoke. And she wasn't even a special friend of mine when I knew her in the old days. In fact she was just plain Else then. But now she insists on being called Elsa. Says it's less German.

I thought they all took Hebrew names, I said.

Edith shrugged. Some of them do.

You were at a low ebb, I said. Besides, she probably meant well.

I'm not saying she didn't.

I think at this point we were interrupted, so I heard the rest of her unhappy story a day or two later.

From what I know about the post-war migrants to Palestine, I suspect that Elsa was acting outside her brief, and knew it. She should have been working from inside the DP camp to

------

which she had been assigned as part of a team, not acting on her own initiative during a brief leave of absence to Berlin. What motivated her: pity for an old acquaintance who was clearly unhappy? Or a less laudable aim, to show off her ability to get things done, change lives for the better? From what Edith told me about her, I have no doubt Elsa was totally sincere about her Zionism. But she must have known that Edith would not be happy in her new environment, that she was the wrong type, the wrong age, not at all the sort of 'human material' they, she and her fellow recruiters, were looking for.

On the other hand, I also know from my recent research that the name of the game in the days prior to 1948 (and indeed ever since) has been first and foremost about numbers. For the moment anyone would do, as long as they were Jewish.

In 1948 I was still an innocent as far as Israel was concerned. It was not a topic that was ever discussed within the family. Even the annual arrival of a box of grapefruit at Christmas did not lead anywhere. Yes, said my father, he had an aunt called Eva in Palestine, and left it at that. He never talked about her, her immediate family, or when they had left for Palestine.

Long before 1948, when Edith arrived, I did know the

story of our escape from Germany, but I also knew that Palestine had never been considered as a possible destination. I knew about the booking to Bangkok in the desperate days following Kristallnacht, but not about my great-aunt in Palestine. Clearly it was never regarded as an option. Was it because we were secular Jews, or because we knew of the existence of hostile Arabs? Whatever the reason, all I knew about Israel when it actually became a reality were the titbits I had picked up from the cinema newsreels. Cheerful propaganda, squeezed in between the Henley Regatta and the latest fashion in hats.

So it was as an almost complete ignoramus that I asked Edith why she had not been happy there. All I had seen were happy, smiling faces, youthful and healthy, rather like Boy Scouts in their khaki shorts, enjoying fresh air and sunlight as they started a new life. Palestine was very much in the news that summer, with the creation of Israel. There were plenty of newsreel stories of happy camp survivors reaching the Promised Land, but no negative publicity. I had never met anyone who had actually been to that part of the world, let alone gone there only to leave. So Edith's evident disappointment really aroused my curiosity.

I thought she might have been homesick, or that she found heat and mosquitoes too much for her. I knew that the living conditions were quite rough, but I did not think, after what she had been through in Berlin, that primitive conditions, even having to sleep under canvas, would have put her off.

To this day I remember what she told me, word for word: Everyone hates everyone else.

I was stunned, and it took me quite a while to understand what she was talking about.

First of all, like so many others, she had been duped into believing that Palestine was 'a land without people for a people without land'. I suspect that Elsa, while not denying the physical existence of a people with a prior claim on the land, tended to belittle the problem. I have since discovered that many of the recruiters who visited camps reported back to say that they considered the inmates to be exhausted by all they had been through, with neither the physical or mental strength to begin their new life in Palestine by fighting a war against the Arabs.

But the Zionists had no option but to take the 'human material' they were offered. This was the best, probably the only chance, to bring their dream of a Jewish state into being. As for the DPs, they were faced with a similar choice, or lack of it. Go to Palestine or stay in the camps.

Edith found herself on a kibbutz. She was supposed to learn Hebrew, but found it hard. Quite a few of the other new arrivals spoke other languages among themselves, but not German, not ever. She did not like taking pot-shots at Arabs, which she was expected to do from time to time.

She was even more upset when she heard stories of British soldiers getting murdered by the Irgun, Begin's resistance movement. Quite early on she began to feel that other members of the kibbutz did not like her, made spiteful remarks about her, often gave her the most unpleasant tasks. Finally someone enlightened her. It was because she came from Germany. She was a *yekke*.

Poor Edith. She had come to Palestine to be among her fellow Jews, this global family, and found herself ostracized because she came from Germany. The word is supposed to originate from the German word for jacket, *Jacke*. Myth has it that German Jews were so posh that they even dressed in town clothes when working in the fields. Underlying the epithet is resentment against a group of people who considered themselves socially superior, were not true Zionists, merely 'Hitler Zionists', and wanted to establish friendly relations with the Arabs.

Take the writer Arnold Zweig, who sought refuge in Palestine but was deeply unhappy. He missed his 'civilized' comforts, was not thrilled at living among Jews (not un-common among people of his social class), hated the narrow nationalism and the insistence on Hebrew. In 1938 he wrote to Freud about Jewish terrorism:

A terrible vengeance will descend upon us all . . . The Jews, who came to this country against the will of the

Arab majority and who since 1919 have been incapable of winning the goodwill of the Arabs, had only
one thing in their favor: their moral position, their pas-
sive endurance. Their aggression as immigrants and
the aggression of the Arab terrorists canceled each
other out. But if they now throw bombs I see a dark
future ahead of us all.

Soon after the war Zweig left for East Germany. Many
'Hitler Zionists' left after the defeat of Germany, as did
Walter Laqueur. The dark future Zweig foresaw is still in the
process of unfolding.

Alison Owing, in her excellent book *Frauen*, about
German women who lived through the Third Reich, recalls
in her introduction a friend 'who returned crestfallen from
a trip to Israel about 1970':

There was so much hatred, she said, hatred among
Jews. She said that because most Israelis had immi-
grated from all over the world, they had little in
common. And *nobody* liked the German Jews. They were
so annoyingly tidy. Sweeping their walks all the time,
watering their damn flowers. They were so *German*.

The British novelist Olivia Manning found herself in
Palestine during the Second World War and much later put

her view of the place into the mouth of a fictional character. It is described as an

> awful place, everyone hating everyone else. The Polish Jews hate the German Jews, and the Russians hate the Polish and the German. They're all in small communities, each one trying to corner everything for themselves: jobs, food, flats, houses. Then there's the Orthodox Jews – they got here first and want to control the show. The sophisticated Western Jews hate the Old City types with their fur hats and kaftans and bugger-grips [sidelocks]. See them going round on the Sabbath trying the shop doors to make sure no one's opened up on the quiet. All they do is pray and bump their heads against the Wailing Wall. Their wives have to keep them. Then all the Jews combine in hating the Arabs and the Arabs and Jews combine in hating the British police, and the police hate the government officials who look down on them and won't let them join the Club. What a place! God knows who'll get it in the end, but whoever it is, I don't envy them.

As early as 1931 a British official wrote: 'What a country – more hatred to the square mile than any other country in the world.'

*

———

Meeting Edith in Berlin, Elsa told her friend what she wanted to hear. It did not need a mind reader to see that she was desperately lonely, had no idea what to do with the rest of her life. Working among displaced survivors in the camps, she had seen it all too often: people with no one to live for and nowhere to go. People who had been through hell and now found themselves unwanted: they needed an aim in life, or they became demoralized and cynical. She and her fellow Zionists knew how to instil hope, and with it the discipline necessary to achieve their ideal, a country made up only of Jews. And if that was not enough to shake Edith out of her depression, there was life on a kibbutz to look forward to.

Imagine, she would have said, looking round the dreary little apartment, you could, if you wanted, never live by yourself again. And she explained the communal system, with its dining room and kitchen, and how even the children were brought up in a collective nursery: so you could look after little children if you wanted to. And no doubt she guessed that Edith, now unlikely ever to have a family of her own, would have been easily seduced by what Elsa was telling her.

If nothing else persuaded her, Edith could not but be seduced by what Elsa told her about life on a kibbutz. She admitted as much when I got a chance to talk to her again.

———

To be honest, she told me, I was frightened at the idea of starting life all over again, on my own, in a strange country. If I had been your age, Eva, it would have been different. I would probably have jumped at the chance, looked on it as an adventure, an exciting opportunity.

I should say! I exclaimed. Anything to get out of Germany.

I opened the biscuit tin, told her to help herself, and stared out of the window. You wait till you've lived through a few English summers. One fine day, to quote Madame Butterfly.

Not surprisingly, the over-used joke was lost on her.

But I'm not young any more. I didn't even know how to restart my life in the flat I'd been given, in the city I'd lived in all my life. But what she told me about life on a kibbutz made it all sound quite different. Wonderful.

I know. I've seen the newsreels. I'm not a Communist, but I think it's a great idea, sharing everything.

I was shocked by the outburst that followed.

It's all lies, she shouted. They didn't want us, any of us, didn't matter where we came from, what we had been through. On the contrary, it was precisely because of what had happened to us that they wanted nothing to do with us. They even discussed building a second dining hall so they wouldn't have to eat with us, the *sabonim*. That's what they called us, *sabonim*, nothing but bars of soap. Because the

Germans are supposed to have made soap out of Jewish corpses.

I was shocked into silence. It seemed beyond belief, such a level of hostility, cruel contempt. In any case it wasn't true, about the soap. Perhaps she had misunderstood? Edith shook her head. I had never seen her look so grim.

In a way I wish they had put us in a different dining room. As it was the *sabras*, the old-timers, always kept themselves to themselves, joking in Hebrew. They would glance across at us from time to time, so it was obvious they were talking about us.

'Us'? So you weren't quite alone.

Yes and no. There was a woman from one of the camps who had lost her husband and two children. She didn't last long, hanged herself in the kitchen one night. And I got quite friendly with a young woman called Marianne, from Breslau, who had been in a labour camp and had nowhere to go now that Breslau was part of Poland. We got quite friendly, told each other things in German when we had a moment to ourselves, which wasn't all that often. But the rest of the newcomers were *Ostjuden*, who spoke Yiddish amongst themselves. They stole things, did hardly any work, and were particularly nasty to Marianne, because she came from a bit of Poland that had been German. They said she wasn't a real Jew, because she didn't keep the Sabbath. Poor Marianne, she got very upset, showed the number tattooed on her arm and said, 'What's that then?' I think she was homesick, not just for her family, all dead now, but for the town where she grew up, knowing she could never go back. All the streets have Polish names now, she said. We'd talk together at night, in a whisper, so nobody could hear us speaking German.

I did not know what to say. Edith was visibly upset, so I kept quiet for a while. The rain had stopped, and pale sunlight broke through before I dared to say anything.

But, I began timidly, I thought the whole point of Israel was to provide a fresh start for Nazi victims, a homeland for those with nowhere to go?

Edith shook her head.

They despised us, she stammered, searching for words. Treated us as though we were scarcely human. Human dust, they called us. I was actually told, more than once, that I had only myself to blame for everything that had happened to me during the war. I should have left Europe, answered the call of Zion long ago. You brought it on yourselves, we were told – degenerates, the lot of you. Servile shopkeepers, traders, alienated from the land that was yours to claim. Some of them even claimed that Hitler had been sent as a punishment. There were remarks about our physique: pale, unhealthy, not fit for the work needed, either to plough the soil or defend it against

———

the enemy. Goebbels had been right to portray us the way he did . . .

Her voice petered out. For the first time since her arrival I looked up to see her crying.

———

What Edith told me about the newly created state of Israel left me puzzled and incredulous. It was such a sweeping, all-embracing condemnation. I do not know what I expected, if anything. Really I was just curious. Now here was a real live Jew who had not only been there but had left it, bitterly disappointed.

Edith sitting in the kitchen, with her sad face, waiting for me to come home from school. Edith waiting for me to grow up and give her a job as my housemaid. I should have understood then what a circuitous, heart-breaking journey she had made to arrive here, back with my family. I was probably too young to appreciate the depth of disappointment that had preceded her arrival. My mother, because of the sort of person she was, could not begin to comprehend the state of mind that had brought Edith back to us. I knew, or thought I knew, that she needed to be part of the family. Having known her as a small child, I thought of her as 'family' anyhow. But sixty years on, I wonder whether any amount of kindness could have compensated for the loneliness at the heart of her existence.

———

I knew too, and knew that Edith must have known, that German Jews had always looked down on *Ostjuden*, the Polish Jews who had flocked to Germany prior to 1933 because it was regarded as the land of culture and economic opportunity. In 1948 I had known this for quite some time because my Aunt Margot had brought disgrace on the family by marrying a Pole, who unfortunately lived up to the stereotype. He had bad table manners, as expected, and also cheated on his wife in a number of ways (not expected). Edith also knew about the Polish Jews, if only because the Nazis started deporting them in 1938, and indigenous German Jews did not always waste much sympathy on them. They were not infrequently blamed for the rise of anti-Semitism.

Perhaps Edith assumed that, after Auschwitz, all such divisions between Jew and Jew would be forgotten. That is what we all assumed. Wrongly, as it turned out. Germans had been good to her, a Russian soldier had embraced her as a fellow Jew. She had pinned too much hope on such isolated incidents. The idea that suffering necessarily improves people is a myth. Take my mother, for example.

When she went underground during the war, Edith took one day at a time, and it gave her an odd sort of strength. There was no point in worrying about tomorrow. If the Gestapo did not get her, an Allied bomb might. Now, with the war over, she had half her life ahead of her: a vacuum.

Elsa seemed to promise what nobody else had been able to offer, a completely new life, a new beginning, and companionship. I doubt whether by this time, if ever, Edith hoped to find a man to share her life with. She had never been particularly attractive and by now she was not even young, on the verge of middle age, which made her situation even more cruel.

Edith had forgotten the lessons that a life of hardship had taught her. The small spites and major hurts of group living in an orphanage. Her stubborn streak had got her through it. Which in turn had perhaps helped to get her through the Nazi terror. But the dream Elsa had promised had let her down. She was the wrong sort of Jew for the Promised Land. Being a *yekke*, snobbish and superior, was bad enough; being a victim was infinitely worse. The New Jew looked like someone out of a Leni Riefenstahl film, handsome in a Hellenic sort of way. The New Jew struck out first, was secretly ashamed of those who had allowed themselves to be killed without a struggle, and so rejected them, even though using them for his own political ends. The ideals of the New Jew who set out to create Israel after the war were remarkably similar to his mirror image, the old Nazi. Not a good omen for the future.

It was no place for Edith. They did not want her, and she did not like what she found. And so, since the future had nothing to offer, Edith wrote to my mother, taking refuge in

———

the past. Britain, as so often, generous to refugees, allowed her to come and work for us in Hendon, in a suburban house with a room going spare. The wrong sort of room, unfortunately, not big enough for her needs. I had guessed as much before she arrived, and I was right.

———

FOUR

———

– 1 –

A lifetime separates the events I have been describing from the present day, a time of recollection. This is not just a personal story, a memoir of private events; it involves what is now history, and our view of important events inevitably changes with the passing of time. It was my misfortune to live through one of the most catastrophic periods in European history. Old age is normally a period of regression, but for people like me remembering brings problems. It cannot be a time of gentle nostalgia. Those who were lucky enough to survive the genocide find themselves having to confront ghosts from the past, lost ones who will not rest in peace, who have no known resting place where we can place our offering, the stone that marks the spot, ensures that the ashes, with the dust of a million others, do not blow in the wind, to haunt us for ever.

The word 'genocide' came into being in 1944, to fill a gap in the civilized world's imaginative landscape, but was left unpronounced for years. It was too impersonal for the world at large, and not personal enough for those of us who had suffered loss. For something like twenty years a veil of

———

silence existed in families like mine, part guilt, part fear at
what we might find if we dared to look. A kind of fascination with the methods of killing, the awful alternatives,
made our situation worse. In the absence of factual knowledge the imagination takes over, and gives us no peace. I
understand what people mean who say, at the end of a
murder trial, that their own sentence is for life.

Most of us are inevitably marked by the trauma of loss,
though the arrival of a new generation – the grandchildren – is unexpectedly healing, even if they do ask
questions, the ones we have avoided facing up to for so long.
Perhaps that is their function, or part of it. Asking the difficult questions. All of them are studying the Third Reich at
school, answering the difficult, underlying questions in
examinations. What Grandmother remembers has become
part of history, and it is, after all, their history too. They
would, as they are very well aware, never have been born if
I had not survived. When they tell me this, I feel happy,
and the last vestige of guilt vanishes.

However, one thing has to be said, cannot be emphasized strongly enough. We did not think of ourselves as
victims. Self-pity was the last thing on our minds. Far from
constantly thinking about the past, most of us were
extremely anxious to put it behind us and move on. I never
thought that I should one day witness a victim culture where
black people compete with Jews in the suffering stakes.

In 1945 the massacre of six million Jews was not considered the most important aspect of the war. Over time that has changed. When Raul Hilberg published the first edition of *The Destruction of the European Jews* in 1961, it had to be sponsored by the Frank and Janina Petschek Foundation. I know, because I was one of the original purchasers, driven by my need to know just how the machinery of mass killing had been organized. Hard to believe now, when Hilberg's book has become an ever-expanding classic. But perhaps not: the Hollywood films and the endless memoirs, quite a few of them fake, are about personal suffering, and do not answer the far more important question so many were asking in 1945: how could Germany, the land that produced Beethoven, descend to this?

The work of Primo Levi also found only a very small readership when it was first published. Now his books do not go out of print. Perhaps what happened was, for a long time, simply too close for comfort, especially taken in conjunction with all the other horrors of the war years. People were tired, they wanted escapism, if anything. Only the young and innocent danced round bonfires on VE night. Even I, at the age of thirteen, had very mixed emotions.

And yet, at a time when public and private life had never been so closely intertwined, I know that the silence observed within the family was matched by public behaviour. As a secular Jew I cannot speak for those who went to synagogue.

They said Kaddish, I presume, but do not know. But as an observant Christian, someone who attended morning assembly at school and, once a month, went to the local parish church as a Girl Guide, I know that no special prayers were offered for the Jewish dead. Nor do I recall my elderly headmaster, who was very given to homilies both in assembly and at a weekly session for sixth-formers modelled on Socrates, saying anything. And nobody among our English friends attempted words of either enquiry or condolence.

What, to be fair, could they have said? All I remember, all anybody remembers, was Richard Dimbleby's famous broadcast from Belsen after British troops opened the gates and were horrified by what they found. The walking skeletons, machines burying emaciated corpses with unceremonious haste. People left the auditorium in silence, and did not utter a word for the rest of the day.

The arguments came later. Could more have been done, should more have been done? Much too late, either way. And perhaps there was a lingering guilt, since Britain had not been immune from anti-Semitism in the 1930s. I got an occasional whiff of it myself in the following years, almost invariably from someone who did not recognize a Jew when they saw one, just as they had been unable to pick one out in Germany – despite Goebbels's odious propaganda, or because of it.

———

The British government knew what was going on – but, for reasons I have never fully understood, kept the facts to themselves. They did not even warn their own troops, who came to 'liberate' the dead and dying, what to expect, and many broke down as a result.

But how do you prepare anyone for something so new, so unexpected? That is the difference between living through events as they happen, and recollecting what has become history, something your grandchildren learn about at school. We have the words now, new dictionaries have been printed, and the dead have been dead for a long time.

Israel has also undergone a fundamental transformation since it came into being in 1948. Edith discovered from personal experience that the *sabra*s did not welcome survivors from Europe with open arms, for the most part treated them with contempt. The New Jew, prepared to fight all comers for his promised land, had no time for victimhood, and yet now Israel has Yad Vashem, where the names of the dead are chronicled and the righteous are honoured. It has a memorial day, when traffic comes to a halt and a silence is observed. Groups of Israelis visit Auschwitz, wearing striped concentration-camp uniforms. Eichmann, who had been living quite openly in South America for years, was suddenly kidnapped by Mossad in 1960 and put on trial in Israel. The notion that finding Eichmann was the result of a long campaign is a convenient myth, recently exposed by

———

someone who knew exactly where to find him, and had tried for some time to get something done about it.

Peter Novick, in his important book *The Holocaust and Collective Memory*, highlights the Eichmann trial as a turning point. Survivors were now encouraged to tell their stories, and the world was ready to listen. Hollywood stepped in, publishers were eager for more memoirs about a period now rapidly slipping into the mists. A small-time crook called Schindler became an international hero. The cult of victimhood was born, and a Swiss musician who called himself Wilkomirski won international fame for his memoir of his early childhood in a concentration camp – before being exposed as a fake. Originally Zionism grew out of persecution, and eventually the new state of Israel had to take on the mantle of victimhood as a form of self-justification, even though it had also fostered the idea of the New Jew, who was tough and aggressive in self-defence. In fact Israel would collapse tomorrow without massive aid from the US.

The creation of most nation-states is a mixture of fact and fiction, myth and collective memory. But the notion of Israel as a safe homeland for Jews is clearly absurd. It is far too small, surrounded by enemies, and most Jews feel safer in Finchley or Manhattan, even if they support Israel and go there for the odd holiday. And then it is not only a racist state, in that you have to be a Jew to live there, but a theocratic one.

The world is full of Jews, and most of them are secular. Hitler would send any Jew to the gas chamber provided just one grandparent was still practising the ancient religion. Forty years of occupation since 1967 (fulfilling Ernest Bevin's predictions of Jewish expansionism) have made a peaceful settlement well-nigh impossible, while the demographic problem refuses to go away. To put it bluntly, Arabs breed at a faster rate than Jews, and the state of Israel now finds itself accepting just about anyone for conversion. And importing Falashas from Ethiopia, a people not recognized as Jews until 1975, when it became expedient to import them.

Almost two decades separate my conversations with Edith about Israel from the Six Day War. In 1967 I had been married and divorced, had two children, and had just published my second novel. I doubt whether I gave much thought to what Edith had told me. If I did, it was probably to assume that the country had then been in its infancy, a melting pot, and that the old divisions between different groups were by now less serious.

Like most people I knew, I was hugely relieved at the outcome of the war. Israel was getting a good press in those days, and though I have always questioned its right to exist, I did think that, provided Israel maintained a position of moral superiority, fulfilled its early promises to share its Western advantages with its Arab neighbours, its continued existence was by now the best outcome possible. Had I known more about Zionism, realized that Israel had another, secret agenda, I would have been appalled. Nobody I knew prophesied that the West Bank would still be under occupation forty years later. But then nobody foresaw the collapse of the Communist bloc, and what could follow.

Year after year I have watched the situation deteriorate, and grown increasingly angry. With the fall of the Berlin Wall any pretence at fairness, justice for the Palestinians, was abandoned. The idea of a Jewish state had always been inherently racist, now it became blatant. An Arab life was worth nothing, while Israel continued to justify its aggressive conduct, its very origins, in the crimes of the Third Reich. Evidence of new waves of anti-Semitism was used to justify Israel and its policies, when in fact the Israelis themselves are largely responsible for arousing hostility to Jews, who often have to defend themselves by explaining that they do not condone Israel's occupation of the West Bank or its murderous treatment of dispossessed Arabs. I myself have been called a Jewish anti-Semite and, yes, a *yekke*, for not supporting 'my people'. I answered that I was British, thank you very much, and that, having had it explained to me many years ago just what a *yekke* was, I was proud to count myself one.

I was remembering Edith and the stories she had told me all those years ago. The ugly divisions were there then and were clearly still present. One story in particular came back to me after I had stormed out of the supermarket, after the above confrontation, not knowing what to do with my anger. His name was Auerbach, according to Edith, and he had got himself into trouble with the Nazis as a left-wing radical even before he was sent to a forced labour camp as a Jew. In

———

the kibbutz, the *sabra*s did not like him, because he had the temerity to voice his opinions at discussion time. Newcomers were expected to shut up, Hitler Jews especially, had to think themselves lucky to be there. But then this cocky so-and-so from Frankfurt had the impudence to argue that it was essential to make friends with the Arabs, or there would never be peace. Apparently he eventually got to the States on some sort of scholarship.

And then I suddenly knew what to do with my anger. Tell the truth. For decades Israel had been exploiting the past, the suffering of people like my grandparents, who would have been appalled to see what atrocities were being done in their name. Decent people like my grandfather, who had crossed out the name 'Israel' on his identity paper before boarding the train to his death, would have recognized the Gaza Strip for what it was, and is: a concentration camp. My grandfather was born in Hamburg, served his country, Germany, in the First World War, and wore a veteran's ribbon in his lapel. What had Israel to do with him, or all the other German-born Jews who suddenly found themselves with an extra name to help identify them?

———

– 3 –

The true story of the creation of Israel is ugly, which is why it has, with time, been conveniently forgotten and replaced by the myth of global guilt at the murder of millions of innocent Jews. It is in fact the story of the thousands of Jews who did not die, because Germany was defeated in 1945 and was unable to finish its self-allotted task of cleansing the world, or at least Europe, of its Jews.

It is easy to mourn the dead. It costs almost nothing and makes those who mourn look virtuous. It is quite another matter to deal with thousands of displaced persons, penniless, often sick in mind or body, who need to be given temporary help and a place they can call home.

Jews.

Jews who through no fault of their own had been uprooted and dispossessed.

Jews who, let us be frank about it, would not be welcomed with open arms by anybody, especially after a crippling war, but who had to go somewhere. It would be America, in the end, who decided what their fate would be,

———

and we have been living with the dire consequences of its decision ever since.

When the war came to an end the Allies found themselves with a problem: thousand of Jewish survivors with nowhere to go. Displaced persons – DPs for short – who had no option but to stay in the camps from which they had supposedly been liberated. Most of them came from what was now the Soviet bloc, where they were not wanted, either by the new regime or by the indigenous population, who had a long history of virulent anti-Semitism and who had usually taken possession of the little property their Jewish neighbours had once possessed. For these Jews going back home was not really an option: there was nothing to go back to except hardship, persecution and hunger.

Dutch Jews went back to Holland, French Jews to France, Italians to Italy. Understandably, very few German Jews wanted to resettle in Germany, despite the material inducements. Some had relatives in Britain or the USA, which made immigration to these countries a possibility. Their relatively high level of education was also a help. It was not unknown for young German Jewish women in the camps to marry their liberators, British soldiers, and start a new life in the UK.

Contrary to popular belief, Holocaust survivors were

not consumed by a passionate desire to reach the Promised Land of their ancient forefathers. They wanted to go where more recent forefathers had wanted to go: America. Driven by poverty and pogroms, that was where the Jews of eastern Europe had been going in their thousands since the nineteenth century. (A few bought tickets to the New World, found themselves in Britain more or less by mistake, and stayed.) Some of these earlier migrants might have heard of Zionism, perhaps even approved of it, but saw Palestine as a destination for others, not for themselves. As for German, Austrian and other west European Jews, they for the most part regarded Herzl as slightly mad, and had no intention of giving up the lifestyle and the civil and political rights they had managed to acquire. British Jews were warned that the creation of a Jewish homeland would become an excuse for anti-Semitism and lead people to question their civil rights as citizens of Britain. This warning was amply borne out by the Third Reich, which was only too happy to collude with early Jewish settlers in Palestine, providing material inducements to encourage German and Austrian Jews to emigrate to Palestine in the 1930s. Eichmann, put in charge of cleansing Austria of its Jews after the Anschluss, even paid a visit to Palestine so that he could personally recommend it to Austrian Jews who came to his office. Even Herzl prophesied that the main supporters of a Jewish homeland would be anti-Semitic regimes, but the prospect did not seem to trouble him. On the contrary.

The fact that Germany had been a land of opportunity for Jews, particularly after 1871, was held against them when times were bad. Envy and paranoia fuelled anti-Semitism after the defeat of 1918, when times were very bad. After 1933 Jews realized, sooner or later, that they would have to leave Germany, and America was the first destination of choice, not just as a land of economic opportunity, but because it was furthest away from Hitler's growing armies. Even the Luftwaffe could not fly that far. The Jews who got out early but settled in France or Holland had made a fatal mistake. Britain at least had the English Channel, and a government which tended to waive the rules on immigration after Kristallnacht.

But the US never changed its rules on immigration, however dire the situation. The quota system that had applied to German Jews before the war, that had many of them waiting in a queue, hoping their number would come up, now applied to the displaced persons stuck in what had been German and were now Allied camps. Only a trickle of Jews from eastern Europe had been allowed in before the war, and only a trickle would be allowed in now. A Hungarian, for example, could expect to wait for ten years.

What was to be done with all these people? Europe lay in ruins. Only the USA, with its wealth, could help rebuild the continent. Britain had put up a gallant fight but, largely as a result of the war, was no longer a world power, and close to bankruptcy. As for the Soviet bloc, officials there were encouraging their remaining Jews to go west and get themselves into the camps, because it was only as camp inmates that the Allies would recognize them as DPs, to be considered for resettlement. So with every passing month the problem grew bigger. What began as an estimated figure of 100,000 was probably nearer 250,000 by the time some sort of solution was on the horizon.

It was a post-war problem which led to considerable friction between Britain and the US, and given the shift in the balance of power in the aftermath of the Second World War the outcome was more or less inevitable – not that the British were blameless in the sorry mess that is the twentieth-century history of Palestine. During the First World War, anxious for allies, they had managed to promise the Promised Land twice over, to the Arabs via the exploits of T. E. Lawrence and to the Jews through the infamous woolly verbiage of the Balfour Declaration, which British administrators of the Mandate realized from very early on was a catastrophic mistake. The explanation for this political blunder seems to be that the British, like so many people before and since, really over-estimated the supposed power and influence of 'world Jewry', this mysterious force for good and evil, mostly the latter, that can cause economies to crash and powerful armies to face inexplicable defeats.

So, with the collapse of the Ottoman Empire, Britain found itself mandated to govern Palestine. It could never have been an easy task, even if no promises had been made.

———

Now the British found themselves increasingly caught between two warring factions, trying to keep an uncertain peace, and a possible target for both sides. On the whole British sympathies were with the Arabs, who had lived in this land since time immemorial and who were now being displaced by European incomers with more money and more guns. Zionism relied on terrorism as well as money, a fact conveniently forgotten by present-day Israeli governments, piously joining in a global 'war on terror'. Today the terrorists are displaced Palestinians.

Nevertheless, Jewish immigration increased between the two world wars, under the British Mandate. With the start of the Second World War, and recognizing Hitler as the greater evil, Jewish terrorists decided to call a truce, even to fight on the British side. Gratitude, however, was not part of the Zionists' long-term agenda. The war was scarcely over when, in 1946, they blew up the King David Hotel, killing more than ninety people. In the following year, as a reprisal for the execution of Zionists, the Irgun hanged two captured British sergeants.

The British, in the aftermath of a long and bloody war, had had enough. So had their government. Washington however, with not a single American soldier committed to keeping an impossible peace between the warring factions, suggesting acceding to Zionist demands by creating a Jewish state in the Middle East. Then all those unwanted, displaced

Jewish survivors could be dumped where they apparently wanted to be. It was by far the cheapest option, would save the need for unwanted immigrants, and would also go some way to appeasing the Jewish lobby back home, a serious consideration with a presidential election on the horizon.

The Americans, who of course had absolutely no official jurisdiction over Palestine, demanded that 100,000 Jews should be allowed to enter the territory in the first year alone, in an attempt to clear the camps. The DPs themselves had no say in the matter: they were told they could either go to Palestine or stay where they were, in the camps. Faced with this choice, which was no choice at all, and encouraged by Zionist recruiters, who at least organized morale-boosting activities designed to prepare them for their new life, it was hardly surprising that so many were willing to risk life and limb in an attempt to reach Eretz Israel, defying British attempts to stop them from landing.

This aspect of the Zionist campaign, backed by the Americans, has been famously encapsulated in the film *Exodus*, the Hollywood version of history based on an atrocious, heavily biased novel by Leon Uris. The ship left Marseilles with 4,500 on board, heading for Palestine. The whole trip had been organized as a propaganda exercise by the Zionists in collusion with the American press, who had been alerted in advance. There was never any question of returning the 4,500 DPs to Germany, and anyone who chose to do so was free to land in France.

But Bevin, on behalf of the British government, was equally determined to take a firm stand when it came to landing in Palestine. The British position was very clear. The Arab population was already up in arms, and the country was simply too small to absorb 100,000 new immigrants in one year, with more to follow. That there would be more to come was becoming abundantly clear. During the period of indecision the numbers involved kept increasing, with new arrivals from eastern Europe infiltrating their way into western camps run by the Allies in the hopes of escaping from Europe to a better life.

Britain and the US could not agree because they had different objectives. Truman, having become President with the death of Roosevelt in April 1945, was first and foremost concerned with getting re-elected. Any decision he made on the homeless Jews stuck in European camps could affect his chances. Allowing mass immigration of Jews would be unpopular with many factions. On the other hand, permitting the creation of a Jewish state in the Middle East would mollify Jewish voters and also please Christian fundamentalists.

The British government, still stuck with trying to maintain law and order in Palestine (with no help from the US), was furious. Bevin's own solution to the problem was to share out the DPs among a variety of different countries.

Bevin never got over his indignation at the willingness of the President and Congress to let the Jewish vote and Jewish contributions to party funds influence their policy on Palestine. Unfairly dubbed an anti-Semite, one remark of his was quoted round the world, to the effect that the American campaign for 100,000 Jews to be admitted to Palestine 'was proposed with the purest of motives. They did not want too many Jews in New York.' In fact what Bevin had said was known to every politician and news-paperman in the US. A year earlier Halifax, then still British Ambassador to the US, had warned him that there was an overriding consensus, if for very different reasons, between Zionists, WASPs and Catholics that the US was no place for Jewish refugees from Europe. But it was something no one could say in public without paying a heavy penalty. Bevin's indiscretion earned him a rebuke from the American press and gave the Zionists all the confirmation they needed to dub him an anti-Semite.

In 1946, at the time of this episode, Truman was in fact neither a convinced Zionist nor committed to the support of a Jewish state. Provided the British administration allowed the 100,000 displaced persons to enter Palestine, he was quite prepared to leave it to the British to sort out the whole

———

sorry mess and find a solution to the problem of Palestine's future. Without offering the services of a single GI.

Recently discovered diaries kept by Truman reveal a level of ranting against Jews which should destroy his image as a philo-Semite for ever.

> The Jews, I find are very very selfish. They care not how many Estonians, Latvians, Finns, Poles, Yugoslavs or Greeks get murdered or mistreated as DPs as long as the Jews get special treatment. Yet when they have power, physical, financial or political neither Hitler nor Stalin has anything on them for cruelty or mistreatment to the underdog. Put an underdog on top and it makes no difference whether his name is Russian, Jewish, Negro, Management, Labor, Mormon, Baptist he goes haywire. I've found very, very few who remember their past conditions when prosperity comes.

Truman was obviously exasperated, and it is a pity that he failed to distinguish between Zionist leaders, an obstreperous minority, and the great majority of displaced Jewish survivors, who wanted nothing more than a quiet life without further persecution. His comments on Jews' behaviour when in power seem prophetic, and it is a pity he did not listen to what seems to have been his gut instinct at the

———

time. The world might have been spared a lot of bloodshed and strife.

By December 1946 there was a certain rapprochement between the US and Great Britain. Truman was more willing to listen to the British problems in Palestine when Bevin came to the White House in person that month with the elections over. Bevin did suggest that if the US increased the quota for entry to the States it would help to alleviate the problem. Truman promised to take up the question with Congress, but nothing changed. Richard Crossman, writing in 1947 about the Quota Act of 1924, put the annual number of the Poles allowed in at 3,000, Hungarians limited to 700 and Romanians to 300; yet the vast majority of Jews now wanting to emigrate originated from these countries.

In an effort to resolve the deadlock on the future of Palestine and the plight of the homeless Jews, an Anglo-American Committee was set up, and a young Richard Crossman, who was to have a very distinguished career as a Labour MP, found himself part of the British delegation. He published his notes and thoughts on the activities of the Committee, and this slim volume very much reflects the British position, and also the resentment felt at the Americans' interference in what was actually none of their business. As Crossman wrote, the future of Palestine either concerned the British, who held the Mandate, or the UN.

Crossman argued, as others had done, that 'Zionist assertions that the Jews *are a nation* are really a reflex of anti-Semitism . . . It is the anti-Semites and racists who want to clear the Jews out of Europe and place them together in Palestine'. More pertinently, he claimed that 'There could not be a worse refuge and home for a persecuted people than this strategic key point in which the whole Arab world is also against them.'

Crossman's book is based on diary notes, so one follows his thought processes almost day by day while the Committee continued in existence. 'As an Englishman,' he wrote, 'I was surprised and irritated during the Washington hearings by the almost complete disregard of the Arab case.' Rather charitably, he puts this down to the 'pioneer' history of America. If the rights of native Americans had been protected by an imperial power, 'half of the USA would still be virgin forest today'. 'Americans,' he mused, 'other things being equal, will always give their sympathy to the pioneer and suspect an empire which thwarts the white settler in the name of native rights.' While Americans are all the offspring of migrants, the British are 'inheritors of unbroken traditions going back for hundreds of years . . . Our instinctive belief is that a nation is a community settled on its ancestral soil.'

Having expressed these rather charitable thoughts on the American psyche, Crossman gives vent to the British anger shared by many of his countrymen:

By shouting for a Jewish state, Americans satisfy many motives. They are attacking the Empire and British imperialism, they are espousing a moral cause, for whose fulfilment they will take no responsibility, and most important of all, they are diverting attention from the fact that their own immigration laws are the basic cause of the problem.

This was not only a Labour opinion. As early as 1945, during the short-lived 'Caretaker Government' before the first post-war election, Churchill wrote in his final comment on the future of Palestine: 'I don't think we should take the responsibility upon ourselves . . . while the Americans sit back and criticise.' By now the Americans were not just criticizing, they were giving orders, making demands. The six British members of the Committee were constantly exasperated by the attitude of the American members. 'Our American colleagues', wrote Crossman, 'held that it was quite unreasonable to ask them to propose active assistance in policing Palestine.' The British people, he wrote, 'felt that it had been very badly used. Ruling Palestine was an unpleasant job anyway, and the British soldier was being

———

forced to do a lot of dirty work because the Americans were inciting the Jews to violence from the sidelines.'

Not surprisingly, the report submitted by the Anglo-American Committee satisfied no one. When its twelve members visited London Bevin had promised that if they submitted a unanimous report he would do his best to get it implemented. As a result the Committee tried to subordinate their differences and concentrate on recommendations upon which they could agree. Palestine alone, they declared, a fact that should have been glaringly obvious even to Washington, could not solve the Jewish problem. Nevertheless, they recommended the immediate admission of 100,000 Jewish refugees and continued Jewish immigration without Arab consent. They opposed partition in favour of keeping a unitary state, but recommended the abolition of land purchases by Jews.

Both Arabs and Zionists attacked the report, and the press on both sides of the Atlantic expressed disappointment at the lack of a clear-cut solution. British politicians, including Churchill, knew that it was vital to get US co-operation, otherwise Britain alone would find itself at war with both Jews and Arabs. Chiefs of staff foresaw an Arab uprising supported by the Arab states, which would require British reinforcements. They suggested asking the US for

———

assistance, or turning to the United Nations. The British Mandate had become a poisoned chalice.

Ernest Bevin, saddled with the problem, was not naïve. By late 1946 there was a general consensus that partition was the answer. Bevin noted that if the idea had been put forward at the end of the war the Zionists would have demanded the whole of Palestine. In fact the leaders of the movement always had a secret agenda, starting with Herzl himself, to expand and get the whole of Palestine eventually, while publicly giving the world reassuring noises about their benevolent intentions towards the Arabs. In June 1895 Herzl wrote in his diaries of the planned displacement and transfer of the Arabs, albeit with financial compensation: 'Both the process of expropriation and the removal of the poor must be carried out discreetly and circumspectly.'

Before the war, the same British official who described Palestine as a country with 'more hatred to the square mile than any other country in the world', as quoted in Sherman's *Mandate Days*, also wrote of the inevitable pressure coming from Europe: 'Every year some Arab sells his land to the Jews. No Jew ever sells his land to an Arab. The Jews are prepared to pay fantastic prices to get land so how can you expect the individual Arab, however "patriotic", to withstand the pressure to sell?'

Ben-Gurion in the 1930s saw partition as a stepping stone to getting all of Palestine. 'A partial Jewish state is not the

———

end, but the beginning,' he wrote to his son Amos, 'a powerful impetus in our historic efforts to redeem the land in its entirety.'

Things came to a head, as far as the British government was concerned, in the bitter winter of 1947. I remember the power cuts, the icy unlit streets, the severe shortage of coal, doing my homework by candlelight in the new house, still in my overcoat. Compared to the war years it all seemed no more than yet another minor inconvenience.

Coal production had always been an essential part of the war effort. Everyone had heard of the 'Bevin boys', conscripts who were sent down the mines instead of going into the armed services, but unless there was a pit disaster mining did not make the headlines. I think I vaguely thought there might be some sort of strike going on – even before the end of the war, but with victory a certainty, there was a feeling in the air, which I picked up from adult gossip rather than anything more substantial, that the workers were getting bolshy. But as far as I was concerned it was just an exceptionally cold winter, with kids sliding on the ice outside the school gates, and I was used to shortages.

In fact, without knowing it, I was living through what was not just a national crisis, but an international one, with far-reaching consequences.

———

———

By the end of 1946 coal stocks had fallen dangerously low, and when the cold weather struck in January not only did power cuts become frequent, but factories began to go on short time. The end of the month saw the coldest night since 1929 and the *Times* headline read ALL BRITAIN FREEZES. Even then no one apparently foresaw either the length of the cold spell or the crippling effect on industry. In February British industrial production was effectively halted for three weeks, and registered unemployment rose from 400,000 to 2.3 million. Floods followed in March, to add to the misery. The situation was worse than anything the Luftwaffe had managed to achieve during the Blitz.

It was a moment of truth both for Britain's self-image with regard to its post-war place in the world, and also for America's view of Britain's ability to cope with foreign-policy commitments. The extent and gravity of the British fuel crisis became a major topic of discussion in Washington, and their gloomy view was confirmed when, in mid-February, Bevin gave notice that the Palestine problem would be handed over to the United Nations. During the freeze-up the Cabinet also agreed to cease aid to Greece and Turkey, withdraw the remaining British troops from Greece, and hand India over to the Indians by June 1948.

Meanwhile I sat in the freezing cold, doing my homework. Still only fifteen, I had passed my General School Certificate with flying colours, for the most part using text-

———

books which ignored the fact that the atom had been split, very publicly, at Hiroshima, and that large areas of pink were disappearing from the atlas. It takes time to bring school textbooks up to date. Besides, there was also a paper shortage.

Berlin, that winter, was even colder, with everything in short supply. There was talk of a 'cold war' too, with the city at its epicentre. But Elsa had persuaded Edith to hand in her keys long before the first snowfall and start the journey to a warmer climate.

5

And so one empire died and a new empire was born. It has not been an improvement. Whatever one might say about British imperialism, it did at least have some knowledge of the territories it administered, and some direct contact with the human beings over whom it had powers of life and death, prosperity or misery. Whatever went on in Whitehall, colonial officials acquired a modicum of understanding for their subjects, and with it came sympathy. After the war a British official wrote that a Jewish state was morally wrong and imperially unwise – 'nevertheless it may now be inevitable after 25 years of drift and pious and rather ineffective well-meaning . . . we have made a most tragic mistake – with untold consequences – in the Middle East'.

The United States, on the other hand, has made a habit of dictating to countries of which it is profoundly ignorant. Financial aid is the carrot, military power is the stick. Rather than engage with real people, it prefers to bomb from a great height. When this is not possible it lands troops, almost invariably with catastrophic consequences. Think Vietnam, think Iraq, plus a lot of lesser skirmishes in between. Any

---

visitor to the US is struck by the insularity of its population, their ignorance of the world beyond its own boundaries.

When Bevin threw in the towel and handed the problem of Palestine over to the UN he was against partition, afraid that the Jews would take over the whole of Palestine once they had increased their population by immigration – precisely what they have been doing ever since 1967. The same fear hardened the position of the Palestinian Arabs. As we have already seen, when partition was considered under the British Mandate during the late 1930s Ben-Gurion was in favour, seeing the proposal as the first step to laying claim to the entire country.

Bevin also feared that the US would support partition but refuse to accept responsibility for implementing it, for the one thing Dean Acheson felt able to say with certainty about American policy was that the US would never allow American troops to be used in Palestine. His fear was fully justified. Israel has illegally occupied the West Bank for forty years and the only power in the world able to do something about it has permitted this injustice to continue. Bevin was also aware that the situation might affect the stability of the Middle East, as other Arab states came to the support of the unfortunate Palestinians. Oil production was also becoming increasingly important in the area.

The partnership between Israel and the US has held for longer than Bevin, who died in 1951, could have foreseen. Military weaponry supplied by the Americans plus a series of humiliating defeats made the Arab leaders less inclined to fight on behalf of their Palestinian brothers. Gushing oil wells meant that Arab rulers who complied with US foreign policy found themselves richly rewarded with useless baubles, golden thrones encrusted with jewels, and private jets. Also a share of weaponry to keep them safe in their palaces. Who, after all, had ever heard of democracy in these countries? Israel, meanwhile, prided itself on being the only democracy in the region.

What nobody seems to have foreseen, at least in the White House, was that gradually humbler Arabs would begin to make common cause with their fellow Arabs, the Palestinians. Television screens showed them the atrocities being meted out in the Gaza Strip, the gradual annexation of the West Bank. On 11 September 2001 the Muslim world finally struck back. Bevin's prognosis was correct, retaliation simply took longer.

In April 1947 Britain asked the UN Secretary General to summon a special session of the General Assembly. This in turn would be asked to set up a special committee to study the Palestine question and report to the regular session of the Assembly. At this special session Cadogan stated that Britain 'should not have the sole responsibility for enforcing a solution which is not accepted by both parties and which we cannot reconcile with our conscience'. A special committee (known as UNSCOP) composed of representatives of eleven states on a regional basis was given the widest terms of reference and required to report by 1 September 1947.

The Committee spent some time in Palestine. The Arab Higher Committee decided to boycott its proceedings. The Zionists, on the other hand, took every opportunity to put their point of view.

By this time relations between Jews and the British verged on war. The objective of the Jewish underground organizations was to wear down the British determination to stay in Palestine, knowing full well that, whatever they might tell the world via their publicity network, the British would not resort to Nazi brutality.

Which brings us back to the Zionists' most famous anti-British propaganda exploit, the voyage of the *Exodus*, a rustbucket expressly named for the occasion. Bevin had made it perfectly clear that the British Navy would not allow the 4,500 illegal immigrants to land in Palestine. He also got assurances from the French that any Jews who chose to return to Marseilles and settle in France would be allowed to do so. As for being 'returned' to Germany, there had never been any intention of doing anything of the sort, but it helped to heighten emotions still further. Only 130 chose to stay in France.

The Zionists had not only forewarned the American press, in fact they colluded with it. They intended to try and land their passengers while the UN Special Committee was in the country. If they succeeded in getting through despite the British patrols it would be a convincing demonstration of Jewish determination. (The Zionist case had always been that all the DPs in Europe wanted to go to Palestine, which was not true.) If, on the other hand, they failed, it would demonstrate British brutality. The Royal Navy boarded the ship off Palestine, and a fight for control – without the use of guns – went on for hours. The captain believed he could beach his ship and get most of the passengers ashore, but he was overruled by the organizers, who told him that the first priority was the political effect of the operation on world opinion. The 'forced' disembarkation of the immigrants on to British ships was witnessed by members of the UN committee and by a large number of American and other journalists. Apart from the 130 who took up the French offer, the rest refused to go anywhere but Palestine. The recent murder of two British soldiers by the Irgun made it impossible to bring any of the refugees to Britain, and no other country would have them. Bevin decided that accommodation for such a large number required territory under British control, and they ended up in Cyprus.

Like many old Hollywood films, *Exodus* gets a regular airing on television. It can only help to foster the myth that Israel came into existence because Jewish survivors would go nowhere else.

Bevin complained that the US government added to British difficulties by supporting and subsidizing terrorism and illegal immigrants. He also emphasized the strategic importance of the Middle East (especially in the event of a war with the USSR) and the need to retain the co-operation of the Arab states. Truman, with an election pending, had already been warned of Arab displeasure by his diplomats. He responded by saying he had no Arab voters.

UNSCOP reported in September 1947 to the Secretary General, and an ad hoc committee of the General Assembly began to discuss it. A majority of UNSCOP (seven out of the eleven members) came out in favour of partition, with Jerusalem under direct UN administration. A hundred and fifty thousand Jewish immigrants were to be admitted in a transitional period of two years, during which the British were to remain responsible for the Mandate. Bevin described the plans for partition as 'manifestly unjust to the Arabs', and the British Cabinet accepted his argument that Britain should decline responsibility for enforcing it.

For the final vote in the General Assembly the US government used all the means at its disposal – including direct intervention from the White House and pressure on client states – to line up the necessary two-thirds majority for approval of the plan. Bevin, angry at the part the US, and the White House in particular, had played in encouraging Zionist claims, instructed the British delegate to abstain. In a Commons debate on Palestine he told the House:

> I think that the Arab feeling in this question has been underestimated. It has got to be assessed at its correct value by everybody, or we shall not get a peaceful settlement. It is because I want it assessed at its proper value that I do not want the Arabs to be dismissed as if they were nobody.

As the situation in Palestine inevitably deteriorated, with rising Arab resistance, the US began to dither in its policy, but Bevin was adamant that the British would withdraw in May 1948. He was bitter about the US: not only were they indifferent to British difficulties, but he also considered them unreliable partners, whose position was liable to shift. Which it did. In March the US delegate to the UN Security Council declared that in view of the deteriorating situation in Palestine 'temporary trusteeship' should be established under the UN. On 14 May the US delegation to the UN, having switched from partition to trusteeship and then to a truce, had just marshalled a majority vote for the appointment of a UN mediator when it learnt over the ticker-tape, along with the other delegates, that a State of Israel had been proclaimed, and that the President had been the first to accord it recognition, sixteen minutes later, without consulting or informing anyone.

6

It is difficult to think of any other political decision taken in the twentieth century that has had such long-term and catastrophic consequences, and all for short-term political ends. Truman got his second term in the White House, and the war continues with no end in sight. The creation of Israel has not been the 'cheap' option it seemed at the time, because US expenditure is massive, just to stop its creation from being wiped off the map. Bevin feared that America would refuse to police the area, by sending in troops to stop Jewish expansion. In fact its behaviour has been far more blatant than anything he could have envisaged at the time. There is no reproof in the form of sanctions, and the United Nations is used as a one-sided tool. Resolutions against the Arabs are piously invoked. Meanwhile the Israelis occupy Arab land, build settlements, carry out political assassinations, use their tanks to mow down women and children, demolish homes as a form of collective punishment, and arrest and imprison democratically elected representatives because their opinions do not accord with their own. People die almost every day on one side or the other, but disproportionately. Ten Arabs for every Israeli is the going rate. When the violence escalates the same proportion holds true. About a hundred Israelis hit by Hezbollah rockets in the north, a few houses damaged or destroyed. In return about a thousand Lebanese, mostly civilians, died. The whole of Lebanon was laid waste, homes, infrastructure, escape routes made impassable. Part of Lebanon had also been occupied by the Israelis for eighteen years, which is how Hezbollah came into being. The Israelis are very good at making enemies, and seem incapable of making friends. Hamas, recently elected by the Palestinians, was also fostered by them in the past. The fact that Hamas and Hezbollah are now beginning to make common cause against a common enemy should give Israel serious cause for concern. Instead it is building new settlements on the West Bank and a wall round east Jerusalem to keep the enemy out. Withdrawing settlements from the Gaza Strip is seen as a big concession. It is nothing of the sort. The idea is to create a giant prison camp for Palestinians, and Israeli troops go in at will to kill its inhabitants as some form of collective punishment. It is as easy as shooting fish in a barrel.

But the world is watching, and does not like what it sees on its television screens. Auschwitz could be kept a secret, but today's crimes against humanity are often witnessed even as they happen. Israel's right to exist is questionable anyhow. The Holocaust was carried out by Europeans, not by Arabs. Its creation by the United Nations was, as I have tried to explain, a dubious exercise, with America pulling the strings. All the six independent Arab states voted against, as did four Muslim countries. Many of those who voted in favour had nothing to lose and something to gain. Either they were client states of the rich and powerful US, or they saw the creation of Israel as absolving them from taking yet more Jewish refugees. Looking at the voting list now, one can only ask by what right Peru or the Philippines or Guatemala should have decided the fate of the Middle East, against the wishes of all those who actually lived there? Geographically, of course, all these countries came under the American sphere of influence.

When Edith arrived in Palestine after the war, she did so in the hope of finding herself among her own kind, one Jew among many. She had found herself discriminated against purely on racial grounds in the country of her birth, and Elsa had persuaded her that all this would be different in the Israel which was about to come into being. Instead she found herself treated with contempt for the very reasons that had brought her here: because she was born in Germany. She was a *yekke*.

As many opponents of the Jewish state had maintained prior to 1948, including Richard Crossman, the Jews were not a nation. They came from different parts of the world, spoke different languages and had different customs. Only the dubious bloodline of race and a few religious beliefs brought them together and, as we all know, the differences that divide people of the same faith can be immense, leading to bitter schisms. The creation of Israel in itself became a bone of religious contention.

The great majority of world Jewry were actually secular, which meant that Israel would not have admitted them, even though the Third Reich killed any secular Jew with one observant grandparent, while Orthodox Jews opposed the creation of Israel on religious grounds.

Less has changed since then than one might at first imagine. Now as then, Israel is still desperate to encourage immigration, since it is engaged in a population competition with Palestinians, who have larger families. There was an influx of Russians once they were allowed to leave the Soviet Union. Then the Falashas, black Africans from Ethiopia, not recognized as Jews until 1975, were suddenly airlifted into Israel a decade later. Now we have Jewish fundamentalists, from Brooklyn or the comfortable suburbs of England, joining settlements on the West Bank, where their existence is heavily subsidized financially, and whom Israeli soldiers are expected to defend. The divisions are deeper than ever, and more fundamental, even if they all speak that concocted language which is modern Hebrew. What is happening on the West Bank is indefensible, and some conscripts are refusing to defend it. The sophisticates of Tel Aviv meanwhile see the settlement of the West Bank as eventually bringing about the end of Israel. The country prides itself on being a democracy, but every government is an uneasy coalition. Even the old boast about 'making the desert bloom' rings hollow as the Palestinians are left without water so that settlers can build showers and swimming pools, as the Jordan runs dry and the Dead Sea turns to salty mud.

How will it all end? Edith, like so many settlers before her, came back to Europe, and ended up telling me her story in our Hendon kitchen, with its indicator which no longer worked, connected to a system of bells which nobody had attempted to operate for decades.

And there she sat, day after day, waiting for me to come home from school, telling me her story, which nobody wanted to hear, except an immature schoolgirl who had begun to learn, the hard way, that life has things to teach us that are seldom in the textbooks (most of which are out of date by the time the world has enough paper to bring them up to date).

I was too young to help her, except by listening when nobody else did.

She continued on her journey, as we all must do. And I, having listened to her story all those years ago, decided it was worth recording. Now, while there is still time.

EPILOGUE

I last saw Edith in a ward of the Samaritan Free Hospital for Women and Children. A great city is like that, if you have lived in it for a long time, as I have: full of unexpected associations which take you back to the distant past. A red-brick, late-Victorian building, it stands on the Marylebone Road and has long since closed. Only the façade, minus its lettering, still stands, like a hollow tooth waiting to be filled, or extracted. Nobody gives it a second glance as they drive past. Only I have cause to remember the building, even though I was only there once. Perhaps just because I never went back a second time.

Edith was homeless yet again, and was waiting, yet again, for someone to help her to make a decision. Who that would be I did not know. It would be someone with authority to sign forms, help her to find work, sort out her legal status as required, perhaps send her back to Germany.

My mother and Edith had parted company without explanation or acrimony. There was a mutual, unspoken understanding between them that things had not worked out, and the fact that Edith needed to have an operation simplified matters. Edith would go into hospital and not return.

I was the only person to visit her in what was a rather gloomy ward. As so often, she was alone in the room, the other beds empty. There were no flowers on the locker, no sign of other visitors apart from myself. She had had some sort of gynaecological surgery: nothing life-threatening, but common enough for women with the onset of middle age. As a schoolgirl I was still fairly ignorant of women's medical problems, and anything she might have told me probably left me bemused rather than enlightened.

I am trying to remember if I brought her a bunch of flowers. I hope I did, since I never saw her again. Perhaps I asked her to keep in touch, but I have no memory of doing so. Now that I have attempted to tell her story the lack of a satisfactory ending troubles me profoundly. The word that springs to mind is *verschollen*, which so often appears beside the names of Jews who died in the Holocaust. Disappeared, missing, lost. But not forgotten.